ROYAL HERITAGE

THE REIGN OF ELIZABETH II

ALSO BY

J. H. PLUMB AND HUW WHELDON

ROYAL HERITAGE

THE STORY OF

BRITAIN'S ROYAL BUILDERS

AND COLLECTORS

1977

ROYAL HERITAGE

THE REIGN OF ELIZABETH II

BY J. H. PLUMB

PUBLISHED IN ASSOCIATION WITH THE

TELEVISION SERIES WRITTEN

BY HUW WHELDON AND J. H. PLUMB

BRITISH BROADCASTING CORPORATION
1981

Published by the
British Broadcasting Corporation
35 Marylebone High Street
London W1M 4AA

Designed by Peter Campbell
Picture research by Desmond Green

ISBN 0 563 17862 0

Printed in England by
Jolly & Barber Ltd
Rugby, Warwickshire

PICTURE CREDITS

Works in the Royal Collection are reproduced by gracious permission of Her Majesty The Queen. For permission to reproduce illustrations acknowledgement is due to the following:
Page 8 photo by Cecil Beaton; 10, 11 Keystone Press Agency Ltd; 13 photos by Cecil Beaton; 18 (right) Crown Copyright, reproduced with the permission of the Controller of Her Majesty's Stationery Office; 18 (bottom left) G. A. Mitchison Esq. of Norman Hartnell Ltd; 22, 23 *Illustrated London News*; 25 Aerofilms Ltd; 26 photo by Cecil Beaton; 27 Fox Photos Ltd; 35 BBC Hulton Picture Library; 37 (bottom) Crown Copyright, National Railway Museum; 46, 47 Keystone Press Agency Ltd; 51 (bottom left) Commonwealth Institute; 55, 59 (bottom) Camera Press Ltd; 59 (top) photo by Les Wilson; 61 (bottom) Giles and Express Newspapers; 62 (top) Norris — *The Vancouver Sun*; 62 (bottom), 63 (top) Jak and the *Evening Standard*; 64 photo by Colin Davey; 92 Feliks Topolski (photos by Marcus Harrison); 93, 94, 95 Feliks Topolski; 103 (bottom) The Trustees of the Estate of Baroness Spencer Churchill; 108, 109 photos by Snowdon; 143, 144 Hamilton Kerr Institute, University of Cambridge; 155, 174 Crown Copyright, reproduced with the permission of the Controller of Her Majesty's Stationery Office.

The photographs of Windsor Castle and Buckingham Palace on pages 52 (bottom), 140 (bottom), 149, 150, 151, 152, 162 (left), 163, 164, 173 (top) and 175 were specially taken by Michael Freeman.

The Coronation photographs on pages 32 and 33 are © BBC. Location photographs taken by BBC staff photographer Joan Williams, © Her Majesty The Queen and the BBC, appear on pages 15, 17, 19, 49, 50, 51, 52 (top), 61, 67–70, 113 (bottom), 137, 158 and 159.

CONTENTS

PREFACE

Without the gracious permission of Her Majesty The Queen to view the extensive royal collections and buildings at Buckingham Palace, Windsor Castle, Kensington Palace, Hampton Court Palace, Balmoral Castle, Sandringham House, and elsewhere, this book could not possibly have been written. For such generous permission, we are deeply grateful.

We are also deeply grateful to Her Majesty Queen Elizabeth The Queen Mother for permission to view Clarence House and the Castle of Mey and Her Majesty's collections and to His Royal Highness The Duke of Edinburgh for his valuable collaboration without which neither the script nor the book would have been written. His Royal Highness The Prince of Wales has also been most generous in helping us in many ways.

As in our previous book, we relied on the generous help of the custodians of the royal collections. Our debt to Sir Oliver Millar, Surveyor of the Queen's Pictures and Mr Geoffrey de Bellaigue, Surveyor of the Queen's Works of Art is immense. Without their active participation, criticism and help nothing could have been achieved. Sir Robin Mackworth-Young, Librarian and Assistant Keeper of the Queen's Archives, was, again, exceptionally generous with his time and knowledge.

We should also like to thank Rear-Admiral Hugh Janion for his kindness and hospitality in showing us H.M. Yacht *Britannia*.

Mr Herbert Lank and the staff of the Hamilton Kerr Institute provided us with exceptionally valuable material on the restoration of royal pictures: and Mr M. D. Tims, Assistant to the Master of the Household, was unsparing in his efforts to help us.

Our thanks are also due to the Lord Chamberlain, Lord Maclean, the Assistant Comptroller of the Lord Chamberlain's Office, Lieut. Col. J. Johnston, the Registrar, Mr Marcus Bishop, and other members of the staff of the Lord Chamberlain's Office, who were tireless in their assistance in making arrangements to visit the collections and in providing illustrations for this book.

In the writing we depended on the assistance of many others, and particularly Miss Ann Turner who directed the programme for which this book was written. J. H. Plumb also wishes to thank his secretary, Mrs Cynthia Levene, for her help and support.

J. H. PLUMB
HUW WHELDON

CHAPTER ONE

THE INHERITANCE

The house in which Queen Elizabeth II was born was blasted into oblivion as the bombs rained down on London during the war; the chapel where she was christened was gutted by the strips of bombs that fell across Buckingham Palace on 13 September 1940 – all, that is, but a fragment that remains as a private memorial to those bitter years. Few monarchs have had so dramatic a childhood as Queen Elizabeth II. Fortunately children can adapt themselves to almost any conditions; all seems natural to them as long as parents and friends surround them. Nevertheless the drama of childhood was important. Until the Queen was ten years of age, there was no certainty that she would inherit the throne. Edward VIII was young, vigorous and very popular; his obsessive love for Mrs Simpson was known to a limited circle amongst whom very few could foresee the tragic outcome – tragic but infinitely providential. At ten, the Queen was old enough to know but not to understand what had happened. Almost before she had grown

Buckingham Palace in wartime. Cecil Beaton's photograph of the Blue Drawing Room

used to the new role of her mother and father, the war broke out and
brought more than a touch of fantasy and strangeness to her life.

She and her sister lived mainly at Windsor Castle, sleeping in the
cellars until a more adequate shelter could be built, but near enough to
London to hear the thud of bombs and the clatter of anti-aircraft guns
and to see the angry glow of the raging fires that might so easily have
engulfed much of her royal inheritance. There was damage – to Kensington Palace as well as to Buckingham Palace, but the great historic
buildings – the Tower, St James's Palace, Marlborough House, Clarence
House, the Queen's Chapel – survived. Even at the Palace of Westminster, the Great Hall of Richard II was not destroyed although the
Commons Chamber nearby was gutted. And the Banqueting House by
Inigo Jones in Whitehall escaped unscathed too.

The war had created almost insoluble problems for the Surveyors of
the royal collections. Buckingham Palace, throughout, remained the
centre of royal authority. King George VI and Queen Elizabeth worked
there day after day: when the blitz was particularly ferocious, they drove
back to Windsor for the night. Bombed or not, they had to work there: as
long as their capital suffered, they could not leave, neither did they want

*A quarter of a mile away
down this tunnel in a Welsh
slate quarry, paintings from
the National Gallery and the
Royal Collection were kept
safely during the Second World
War. The container holds
pictures being taken to the
studio set up nearby for
cleaning and restoration*

Lord Clark examining paintings from the Royal Collection in storage in Wales. On the wall above him hang Rembrandt's 'Lady with a Fan', Jan Steen's 'The Morning Toilet' and Vermeer's 'Lady at the Virginals'

or intend to, they and their people endured all that Hitler could send. The great functions of monarchy could not cease – the reception and entertainment not only of exiled governments and statesmen but also heads of allied government and sometimes their wives. Queen Wilhelmina of the Netherlands arrived with only the clothes she was dressed in; other monarchs were scarcely better provided for, but the King and Queen always rose to the occasion, providing comfort and hospitality. Mrs Roosevelt, a very welcome friend, also made a short visit. She was, of course, commodiously provided for – except that the windows had been blown out and were fitted with temporary shutters, and the bitter draughts were not greatly alleviated by the one very small electric fire. In fact Mrs Roosevelt had the Queen's own bedroom.

Such visits and the continuing royal presence meant that furniture and pictures had to be kept at the Palace and were thus at grave risk. In any case it was impossible to strip every royal palace of every stick of furniture, every painting and drawing, all the sculpture, bronzes, china, silver and armour. Both Hampton Court and Windsor were considered reasonably safe. The great Picture Gallery at Buckingham Palace, with its exceptionally fine Rubenses and Rembrandts, was emptied and sent off to Wales with the finest paintings from the National Gallery, under the care of Lord Clark. Others were sent down to Windsor to be kept in the cellars there. Safe space was difficult to secure but disused parts of the

Underground were commandeered. Five large cases of china (possibly including the beautiful Chelsea service commissioned by Queen Charlotte, the wife of George III, for her brother) were tucked away at the Old Knightsbridge station and then later moved to a more secure part of the Underground at Aldwych. Much of the Palace had an air of oddity, all cupboards with glass doors being turned to face the wall to diminish the risk of blast. In order to keep a visual record of what was done, Queen Elizabeth asked Cecil Beaton to take a series of photographs. Although Windsor Castle remained less affected, even there some of the great chandeliers had to come down, and the rarest pictures – the Holbeins, the Vermeer, the great series of Lawrences and many others – could not be left at risk. Even at Windsor, therefore, where the princesses lived, there was some sense of vanished splendour, except in the rooms used by their parents – which, of course, underlined the contrast. And with the distant sound of bombing, anti-aircraft fire and the burnt out ruins which the princesses saw on their weekly visits to London, there was a constant reminder of the war's destruction.

The war years took their toll in other ways. Only the minimum of work of maintenance could be undertaken: paint peeled, stucco crumbled, furniture decayed. Every year the backlog of essential needs grew longer and longer. To war damage was added necessary neglect.

The least affected of all royal residences was Royal Lodge at Windsor where the King and Queen had lived before coming to the throne and for some time afterwards. Indeed, they had been responsible for retrieving it from decades of neglect and turning it into a beautiful country home. They became so deeply involved that they commissioned Sir Owen Morshead, the Royal Librarian, to write a history of all that they had done. The princesses had spent the first year of the war at the Royal Lodge, where their parents had created the most aesthetically satisfying background the princesses enjoyed during their early years. Both parents were passionately interested in the artistic quality of their surroundings: their mother, as well as possessing infinite charm and grace, has a most discerning eye. Both she and King George VI loved gardens as well as buildings and they gave a great deal of thought not only to the restoration of the Lodge but also to its setting.

George VI was a far stronger and far more gifted character than many of his subjects realised. There has been a tendency to highlight his occasional error of judgement, such as his preference for Lord Halifax rather than Winston Churchill as Prime Minister in 1940. People forget that Churchill had been one of the most passionate supporters of Edward VIII's desire to marry Mrs Simpson. The King was criticised, almost

Buckingham Palace stripped down for war. These pictures taken by Cecil Beaton show damage done to the Chapel (top left and bottom right) and empty frames and blocked up doorways in the West Gallery (top right) and the Picture Gallery (bottom left)

mocked, for his obsessional preoccupation with the niceties of official dress and decorations, but a sharp and critical eye will notice such things: they jar aesthetic sensibility. The King was a deeply dedicated man, as dedicated as his father or great-grandfather to the dignity of the throne and its ideal of service. He also possessed a fine eye and excellent taste. Aesthetic judgement does not necessarily go with a profound knowledge of the history of art or with a passionate commitment to modern trends in aesthetic expression, but he was sensitive to the making of landscape, to the subtlety of green in changing light, from the yellow to the blue. He had a true instinct for placing a bush or a tree and he responded to the beauty of flowers. Indeed, both he and Queen Elizabeth were natural gardeners as the perfect setting which they created for Royal Lodge clearly demonstrates. No swimming pool could be more cunningly hid. And the charming tiny house, 'Y Bwthyn Bach', which the people of Cardiff had presented to Princess Elizabeth and in which she and her sister loved to play, was given its own miniature yet exquisite garden.

Not only gardens exercised the royal eye. When, at his suggestion, the George Cross was created as an award to civilians for gallantry – the VC could only be given for gallantry on active service – the King himself designed it. Orders fascinated him, as they fascinate many, for their beauty, for their ability to convey so much in miniature. As well as being drawn by their beauty, his deep sense of order was gratified by carefully arranging the great collection of stars, ribbons and collars, many of which had been given to his father and grandfather, in cases in the Long Corridor at Windsor Castle. His quick eye also noted how the arrangement of the beautiful oval portraits by Gainsborough of the children of George III could be improved. Over the course of time they had been jumbled up and their sequence bore no relation either to their ages or the way Gainsborough wished to display them. George VI worked out the Gainsborough sequence and they were rehung in that order in the Long Corridor at Windsor.

George VI's aesthetic interest was aroused by more than gardens and the arrangement of outstanding works of art; he was also a distinguished embroiderer, a skill which he shared with at least one of his Field Marshals. Such careful, dedicated work as embroidery drives the mind away from problems and anxieties, creating a comforting concentration. The worries and burdens of the war and its aftermath weighed very heavily on the King. His *gros point* embroideries, which afterwards covered the seats and backs of many of the chairs in the Drawing Room at the Royal Lodge, were an anodyne in those anxious years. They blend perfectly in that beautiful neo-Gothic room, first created by George IV,

A chair cover embroidered by King George VI, from a set in the Drawing Room, Royal Lodge, Windsor

with its soothing vista of the garden beyond the high windows.

It is important to stress the perceptive and discerning eye of George VI – an eye that was very much in action, too, either in stalking deer or in shooting game – because so many have dismissed or ignored this side of his personality. The Queen did not grow up in a family atmosphere that was indifferent to art or to beauty not only of nature but of things. Even if her father had been totally indifferent, her mother's interests were sufficiently strong to impart a love of beauty, and a deep and abiding care for her inheritance.

Queen Elizabeth, the Queen Mother, possessed knowledge as well as an instinctive flair for works of art. Naturally her tastes and discernment were encouraged both by her surroundings, living as she did amidst one of the greatest collections of art in the world, and also by her family. She herself has formed one of the most delightful small royal collections, putting together a number of important modern pictures that now adorn the walls of her home at Clarence House as well as at Royal Lodge. There are Impressionists – a very beautiful Sisley and a striking Monet – and one or two Old Masters, but the strength of the collection lies largely in contemporary British painters in whom George VI also took an interest. One picture which I find constantly a surprise for its sharp visual impact (like a phrase in music, it can haunt the mind) is Sir William Nicholson's *The Gold Cup*, painted in 1937. Nicholson was an underrated painter, and the picture of a *Woman with a Glove* in the Fitzwilliam Museum, Cambridge, is equally haunting, though for very different reasons. There is also a most unusual L. S. Lowry, bought long before he became so fashionable, a fine Matthew Smith, good Sickerts and Sargents and, perhaps rather surprisingly, a splendid Augustus John portrait of that old iconoclast, George Bernard Shaw. Some of the most moving pictures at Clarence House are those which John Piper painted of Windsor during the war: the skies are storm-ridden with scudding clouds, and even more ominously the quadrangles and courts, usually crowded with people, are empty and forlorn.

Naturally the Queen Mother has always been eager to acquire pictures that relate to her ancestors, particularly the Scottish branch of the Royal Family, the Stuarts, of which she has acquired many attractive portraits. Her other great interest – racing – is well represented in a number of excellent sporting pictures. The horse captivates anyone with a discerning, aesthetic eye.

Pictures, however, form only a part of her aesthetic contribution. She creates an extremely personal style in her homes which is particularly apparent in the decorative effects that she achieves with china. She has formed a small but very fine collection of Chelsea, of which the outstanding pieces are plates decorated with botanical paintings, a part of a service named after Sir Hans Sloane who ran the physic garden at Chelsea in the early eighteenth century. On the wild north coast of Scotland, at the Castle of Mey which she saved and restored, there is a collection of Wemyss china – a Scottish pottery whose great days were in the late nineteenth and early twentieth centuries. The painting is very bold: cherries, plums, strawberries or flowers – irises, daffodils, dahlias and, frequently, roses; the decoration is very reminiscent of early Chelsea. Years after the Queen Mother developed an interest in this pottery, it is now keenly sought by collectors throughout the world.

It is important to stress the Queen Mother's artistic interests, and particularly her sharp eye for arrangement, for this was a formative influence on the young princesses in their early years and when they came to womanhood after the long years of war. There was also one other important influence on the Queen which has a bearing on both royal buildings and collections: she learned a very great deal from her grandmother, Queen Mary. No one could suggest that King George V had the

'Y Bwthyn Bach', the miniature Welsh cottage in the grounds of Royal Lodge, was a surprise gift to The Queen when she was Princess Elizabeth of York, made in 1931 by the Lord Mayor of Cardiff in the name of the people of Wales. In April 1980 the Queen watched with the film cameras while her grandson, Master Peter Phillips, explored for the first time this delectable house built and furnished to a child's scale

The sitting room has a portrait of the Queen Mother when she was Duchess of York, a Welsh dresser and the table laid for a dinner-party. In the kitchen (left) all the appliances work, and the electricity meter cards from the 1930s still hang over the stove. Upstairs, there are a bedroom, and a bathroom complete down to a miniature tin of cleaning powder. The present 'custodian' of the cottage for the Royal Family is Lady Sarah Armstrong-Jones

The Armills or 'Bracelets of Sincerity' (above) were specially made for the 1953 Coronation and were a gift from the Dominions. Although armills still exist from the regalia of Charles II, this was the first time that such bracelets had been used in the actual ceremony since the coronation of Queen Elizabeth I. From ancient times armills had been a symbol of royalty and held especially sacred. It was on a bracelet that the Danes swore to keep the peace with King Alfred. In 1953 the armills were placed on The Queen's wrists by the Archbishop of Canterbury with the words 'Receive the bracelets of sincerity and wisdom . . . for symbols and pledges of that bond which unites you with your people'. Many who were watching television will also remember the moment when The Queen appeared on the balcony of Buckingham Palace after the ceremony and the four-year-old Prince Charles momentarily forgot the crowds in his curiosity over the armills

Caddinets were originally place settings for grand banquets; these made for William III and Mary II have been acquired recently and are displayed at the Tower of London. At the 1953 Coronation a similar caddinet was used as a portable desk during the signing of the Oath

In earlier rituals armills were tied to the 'Stole Royale' which dates back to the ceremonial robes of the Byzantine Emperors and was copied in Coronation rituals by medieval monarchs throughout Europe. The embroidery on this modern stole (top left) and The Queen's Coronation Dress (below left) included the emblematic flowers of the Commonwealth: the wattle for Australia, the fern for New Zealand, the maple leaf for Canada, with the rose of England, the thistle of Scotland, the leek of Wales and the shamrock of Ireland

Clarence House, the London
residence of Queen Elizabeth,
the Queen Mother.
Top: Morning Room
Left: Hall

least interest in art, outside a good likeness in a state portrait or a fine head on a stamp. There is, indeed, a famous story that when he was visiting an art exhibition he called to Queen Mary, 'Come over here, May, there's something which will make you laugh.' He was looking at a Cézanne! And yet stamps, which can be very beautiful works of art in miniature, entranced him. Nor was Queen Mary interested very much in painting, unless it was a portrait of an ancestor, but she loved objects: hardstones – jade, rock crystal, rose quartz; china, of course, of every sort and variety; Fabergé almost as much as her mother-in-law, Queen Alexandra; small pieces of silver work (not that she was indifferent to large ones); ivories, particularly Indian; boxes – gold, silver, mother-of-pearl, ivory; bibelots, étuis, nécessaires. Small objects of high craftsmanship delighted her. Her rooms at Marlborough House, where she lived in her widowhood, were full, almost crammed, with the collections of a long lifetime. Such an inveterate, unstoppable collector was inevitably deeply interested and deeply concerned with the royal heritage of buildings and with the artistic treasures with which she lived, and her knowledge of them was greater than many of the Surveyors who served her. Furthermore, Queen Mary possessed an orderly mind and so she kept careful catalogues of her multitudinous collections in three very large volumes. She knew the importance of scholarship (even if on occasion she made mistakes), and of authenticity (even if she inclined, as all collectors will, to optimism). These matters were also, as she realised, of supreme importance to all royal collections, and she was deeply disturbed by the confusion in which the Duke of Cambridge left his. And it is probable that this insistence on scholarly care, of accurate records, has influenced the Queen's attitude to her inheritance.

And her inheritance was incomparable: the Vatican might rival its Old Masters; the Royal House of Denmark might almost match the collection of china; the Royal House of Orange once possessed, maybe, a finer Rembrandt, a finer Hals and, at least, one finer piece of gold plate; the Royal House of Spain certainly had incomparably greater Spanish, Flemish and Italian paintings (some, alas, formerly in possession of Charles I); but only the very greatest museums – the Louvre, the Metropolitan Museum in New York, the National Gallery and the Victoria and Albert Museum in London – surpass the Queen's collections in quality and range. If all the Queen's collections were placed in one building, it would take its place immediately as one of the most outstanding museums in the world.

The royal heritage has grown over the centuries like some great coral reef. The Tower, the oldest of royal palaces, first built by William the

Gainsborough's portraits of George III and his family in the Long Corridor at Windsor Castle. Queen Victoria had had them hung separately and it was King George VI who restored the artist's grouping of the portraits by age and in three rows with frames touching

SHARING LONDON'S LOT: THEIR MAJESTIES VIEW THEIR DAMAGED HOME.

THEIR MAJESTIES INSPECTING THE DAMAGE TO BUCKINGHAM PALACE AFTER THE EXPLODING OF THE DELAYED-ACTION BOMB ON SEPTEMBER 10.
NOT A PANE OF GLASS WAS LEFT INTACT IN THE NORTH FRONT, WHERE BOTH THE KING AND QUEEN'S APARTMENTS ARE.

THE EFFECT OF FUTILE AND BARBAROUS VIOLENCE DIRECTED AGAINST THEIR MAJESTIES' PERSONS: THE HISTORIC CHAPEL AT BUCKINGHAM PALACE
WRECKED BY A BOMB DELIBERATELY AIMED AT THE MOST FAMOUS ROYAL RESIDENCE.

When bombs were scattered indiscriminately over London, one fell at the corner of the north and west fronts of Buckingham Palace, and blew up on the morning of September 10. The King and Queen were not in residence, and no one in the Palace was hurt. The bomb landed near the Queen's sitting-room on the first floor. The windows of the room were shattered, the doors were damaged, the plaster of the ceiling fell in, and the floor was covered with glass and debris. Later, the Palace was deliberately bombed, and the chapel and the Queen's apartments damaged. *(Photographs by Wide World and G.P.U.)*

Pages from the 'Illustrated London News' of 21 September 1940 and 28 October 1939

ROYALTY AND THE RED CROSS: THE QUEEN'S PALACE SEWING-PARTY.

A BI-WEEKLY SCENE IN THE BLUE DRAWING-ROOM AT BUCKINGHAM PALACE : HER MAJESTY AT ONE OF THE WORK-TABLES ROUND WHICH MEMBERS OF THE ROYAL HOUSEHOLD MEET TO MAKE CLOTHES AND SURGICAL DRESSINGS.

Since the outbreak of war none have shown themselves more tireless and inde-fatigable in Britain's cause than the King and Queen. Some of their more recent self-imposed tasks, carried out by their Majesties jointly, are illustrated on another page. Here the Queen is seen working among wives of members of the staff of her own household at Buckingham Palace. While her Majesty herself is busy sewing, other helpers at the two tables are knitting or winding wool. The contrast between the marble columns round the walls of the blue drawing-room and the plank trestle-tables is typical of wartime adaptations. (L.N.A.)

Conqueror, had been added to throughout the long middle ages. Everything was done to make it commodious, up-to-date, liveable, even including newfangled chimneypieces, but it remained a fortress, a grim reminder of the feudal age. Henry VIII was the last King to attempt any major building; after the Tudors, no monarch lived there. Hampton Court and St James's Palace were built and loved by the Tudors. The Stuarts were indifferent to St James's but it found favour again with the early Hanoverians; George III, however, detested it. He bought Buckingham House and lived there: his son turned it into a Palace. Windsor enjoyed a love-hate relationship with the monarchy stretching over the centuries but, unlike the Tower, the Castle became steadily less fortress-like and more domestic. Queen Victoria disliked Buckingham Palace and, after Prince Albert's death, Windsor; and Prince Albert built Osborne and Balmoral and bought Sandringham for their son, the Prince of Wales. Kensington Palace attracted William III who bought it; George I and his son George II enjoyed living there but almost no one else did. George III was the only monarch to live for a time in the Dutch House at Kew, its exceptional gardens were started by his parents. In Scotland, there was the Palace of Holyroodhouse, dragged back to life by King George V and Queen Mary who thought that it was high time that the British monarchs had a formal palace in their Scottish capital – and what better than the great palace of the Stuarts in the heart of Edinburgh. There are other royal palaces and castles in Scotland – Stirling, Linlithgow, Falkland – which have passed, as it were, on permanent loan to the Scottish people. Linlithgow is a ruin but Falkland and Stirling still endure.

Like all great estates, there are smaller outlying houses. At Windsor, there is the Royal Lodge, now used by the Queen Mother. In the Park also stands Frogmore, which is not used except for an occasional tea-party. Frogmore lacks central heating and lives up to its name – it stands on a dark and marshy piece of the Park. Architecturally, it is a fine house: Queen Victoria's mother lived there, and the books Queen Victoria used as a child are still there as well as some very fine Wedgwood china. The garden, designed by Sir Uvedale Price, is a small oasis of privacy at Windsor. Within a stone's throw of Buckingham Palace there are three fine houses – Lancaster, Marlborough and Clarence House: the first is now given over to government functions – conferences, receptions and the like, the second to the Commonwealth Secretariat, and the last is, of course, the Queen Mother's London home. At Sandringham there is York Cottage – very small, unbelievably small when one realises that George V lived there as Prince and King with all of his children for

Windsor Castle from the air, looking south-east. This photograph was taken in 1947 before the replanting of the Long Walk (right), which had been planted in Charles II's reign and cut down in the 1940s. In the centre is the Frogmore Mausoleum with (left) the square of Victorian greenhouses and vegetable gardens

*George VI took a special
interest in the royal estates –
a photograph taken in 1942*

decades; that Queen Mary had most of her children in the tiny bedroom
there. Where their little court lived and slept is a mystery. The Cottage
is scarcely larger than a Wimbledon villa, which indeed it much re-
sembles, and is now used as the Estate Office. At Balmoral there is
Birkhall, a lovely small house with a beautiful garden that dips away
sharply from the house: when the house is discreetly out of sight, it
bursts into a riot of vegetables. More attractive still are the little houses
that Queen Victoria built deep in the mountains so that she might be
alone, either with the Prince Consort or to brood on her loss after his
death.

It seems a vast number of houses for one family, and certainly learning
even the geography and topography of Windsor Castle alone must have

*Queen Elizabeth with Princess
Elizabeth and Princess
Margaret – a photograph
taken at Windsor by Cecil
Beaton in 1942*

been admirable training for the royal memory, but in fact there is a considerable illusion in this recitation of royal residences. The Tower and Hampton Court contain large museums; St James's many offices; indeed, that is true of a great deal of Buckingham Palace, for the Queen and her family live only in a part of it. Osborne has been given to the nation; much of Windsor is open to the public. The only two houses which the Queen enjoys, as it were, in their entirety are Balmoral and Sandringham, which are private residences. Many of the royal palaces – St James's, Hampton Court, Kensington, for instance – also contain flats and apartments for other members of the Royal Family and for those courtiers whose duties involve them closely, and on a daily basis, with the monarchy.

Nevertheless, the royal space is vast and it is furnished space. Like the houses and palaces, the royal collections were accumulated over the centuries, sometimes slowly, sometimes in almost a tidal wave. Of the Royal Family's medieval inheritance, apart from the Tower and Windsor, very little remains in the royal collections. There are, of course, buildings, many of them that were once royal – the great castles of Wales, the palace at Eltham, and important vestiges of the Palace of Westminster – the Jewel House, the Great Hall of Richard II, the crypt of St Stephen's – which still technically belong to the Crown. But for the stupendous gift of the old Royal Library by George II as a foundation present to the British Museum, the monarchy would possess one of the finest collections of illustrated manuscripts and medieval music in the world.

The present collection really begins with the Tudors. Some of the earliest pictures are portraits. From the fifteenth century onwards portraits of prospective brides, or bridegrooms for that matter, were exchanged when a royal marriage was contemplated. Some of the earliest pictures derive from this custom. The Tudors also began to put together portraits of former Kings and royal portraits have always been an important part of the collection. Henry VIII, too, commissioned pictures of the great diplomatic events of his reign – the meeting with the Emperor Maximilian or the famous encounter with Francis I of France at the Field of the Cloth of Gold. Equally important are the beginnings of the great collection of armour which date from Henry VIII's reign and include his own terrifying suit. Throughout the Tudor period portraits began to accumulate and the nucleus of the great miniature collection (now the largest in the world) starts in the reign of Elizabeth I who discussed the art with Nicholas Hilliard, the greatest miniaturist of her time.

The collections, however, begin to burgeon and swell with the

Charles I, the first great royal collector. This portrait, by Daniel Mytens, is a recent addition to the collection

TEMPERANCE *enjoying a Frugal Meal*.

Caricatures of George III and his son by Gilray. Their real characters showed in the contributions to the royal collections for which they are probably best remembered — the books (now in the British Library) of the former, and the Pavilion at Brighton of the latter. These prints are from the collection in the Royal Library, Windsor

A VOLUPTUARY *under the horrors of Digestion*.

Stuarts. Charles I was an aesthete in its deepest and best sense. He patronised Rubens and van Dyck as well as many other artists. He bought
the splendid Mantegnas now at Hampton Court: indeed, at the time
of his execution, his collection of paintings was one of the most outstanding in Europe. Alas, it was auctioned off by Parliament and dispersed;
but a large number of his paintings had not been sold or had not gone
abroad by the Restoration. A few, like the Mantegnas, were retained by
Cromwell; some were returned immediately at the Restoration, and
others were purchased later. There were great losses, it is true, but the
core of the Royal Collection is still impressively Stuart, for Charles II also
bought pictures, furniture, silver and possibly, but no one knows when
or how, the exceptionally fine series of drawings by Leonardo da Vinci.
William III, a neglected monarch in every way but a man of taste and
discernment, made very considerable contributions in furniture, pictures
and buildings; his wife, Queen Mary II, began the great collection of
pottery and china, with the brilliant Delft-ware that now adorns Hampton Court and elsewhere.

The Hanoverians, apart from George I whose contributions were
largely architectural or concerned with gardens, added more to the
collections even than the Stuarts. This is particularly true of Frederick,
Prince of Wales, the father of George III, of George III himself, and of
his son George IV, who rivalled Charles I in his dedication to the arts.
Frederick was responsible for adding some fine Old Masters, both paintings and drawings; George III bought a large collection of Canalettos, as
well as important Old Masters, from Consul Smith of Venice in 1762 in
order to adorn his new palace at Buckingham House. He also patronised
the finest English craftsmen and, although not a great deal remains, he
added considerably to the furniture collection. He began collections of
his own. He was a compulsive bibliophile, as obsessive in buying books
as any chain-smoker in purchasing cigarettes, and he loved clocks,
watches, scientific instruments and much else. Although his huge library
– or most of it – was given by his son to the British Library in exchange
for cancelling some of his mountainous debts, his other collections
remain – including his own Observatory at Kew.

George IV, however, surpassed his father as a collector. He could do
nothing by halves whether it was falling in love (which he did frequently
but always totally) or buying scent by the quart or handkerchiefs by the
gross. He bought from earliest youth to old age, never caring much about
the debt – a splendid example of private indulgence becoming public
benefaction. He acquired a very large number of fine Dutch and Flemish
pictures – wonderful Rubenses, brilliant Cuyps, fine Potters (including a

splendid one now in the Queen's sitting-room at Windsor), Jan Steens which can be read as Dutch morality stories or simply enjoyed as beautiful pictures, Rembrandts (including one of the Queen's favourite pictures, *The Shipbuilder and his Wife*), and many, many more. (Of course, in his torrent of purchases he managed to acquire a few fakes, including a bogus Rembrandt.) He was also a very great patron of contemporary painters, particularly George Stubbs and Sir Thomas Lawrence. He bought and commissioned furniture with the same verve, and took delight in regimentals – so in came firearms, swords, prints, drawings of military life. And to him, and almost to him alone, is the Royal Collection indebted for its unmatchable collection of eighteenth-century French porcelain and furniture.

By the time of his death in 1830, the royal collections were vast. Queen Victoria married a prince whose taste, though less ebullient than George IV, was nevertheless profound. Albert loved pictures, particularly of the early Renaissance. He was a great patron, too, of artists of his day – particularly Winterhalter and Landseer. Science and all types of new technology fascinated him as well, and the Royal Collection of photographs dates from the very earliest days of photography. Indeed the first English news photograph – the Chartist meeting in 1848 on Kennington Common – is in the royal collection.

By Victorian days the royal collections were at a flood-tide and only a few tributaries have seeped in since. The most important, perhaps, is the great collection of stamps created by George V and extended by George VI. There have been other smaller additions – the Fabergé that Queen Alexandra and Queen Mary loved so much, and, of course, Queen Mary's own collection of hard stones. In essence, however, the royal collections had reached their major extension by the end of the nineteenth century, if not somewhat before; indeed the death of Prince Albert in 1861 could mark the end of major growth.★

If the days of the Queen's adolescence were made dramatic by war, the years of her early womanhood were bleak. The hopes that victory engendered were quickly transferred into the realities of peace. As the forties dragged on to a close, the years were hard and grey. People were no longer bombed; the sailors, soldiers and airmen came home promptly; but the country remained deeply scarred. There was a burnt-out desert around St Paul's and flourishing trees grew in the heart of the City. Like England, Europe too was littered with destruction: tiny prefabricated

★For the detailed story of these collections see *Royal Heritage: The Story of Britain's Royal Builders and Collectors* by J. H. Plumb and Huw Wheldon (BBC Publications), and Oliver Millar, *The Queen's Pictures* (Weidenfeld and Nicolson and BBC Publications).

Frames from the filmed recording of the BBC's television broadcast of the Coronation.
Top: Arrival of The Queen's procession in Westminster Abbey
Bottom: The moment of crowning

32

houses huddled near mountains of rubble. The great rivers were bridged by floating pontoons; trains crawled over temporary viaducts; roads were battered with the craters of war. Hunger was everywhere: hunger and hopelessness. And fear. The precarious, half-fictitious democracies of Eastern Europe collapsed one after another, caught in the stranglehold of Russian communism. As after World War I, the Kings departed; an iron curtain cut the West from the East.

In England there was little euphoria of victory: shortages of food got worse, for a time even bread was rationed. A Labour government tried to build a welfare state and ran immediately into chronic economic problems that led to devaluation, inflation, the spectre of unemployment and decay. The Empire was in no better shape: draconian measures – the division of a continent into India and Pakistan – led to appalling religious wars; Burma vanished into socialism, poverty and obscurity; Africa and the Caribbean grew restive. The future of the Empire looked as bleak as the economy. Only the institutions of government seemed firm and rocklike. George VI, a dedicated constitutional monarch, was determined to work with scrupulous impartiality with all political parties, so the misgivings of the left-wing socialists such as Sir Stafford Cripps soon turned into real admiration for the King and for Queen Elizabeth whose grace and charm gave a radiance to life in the greyest years. In a crumbling world at least monarchy and parliament seemed as secure as the Rock of Gibraltar, but little else, and few would have predicted the future even for them.

In 1950 the fatigue of the country, its longing for more – more almost of everything – nearly toppled the Labour government; at a general election Clement Attlee scraped back into power with a majority of three. In 1951, his nerve gave and Sir Winston Churchill took back the reins of government. Although there was a violent and dangerous war in Korea, Europe itself was clawing its way back to prosperity – even in Germany the rubble was going; in France the scars were healing; in England there was a perceptible lift in the economy. A hint of dawn was in the air when disaster struck the Royal Family. On 6 February 1952 King George VI was discovered dead in bed: he had died during the night of thrombosis brought about by a major operation for lung cancer the previous year. And so a young, a very young, Queen came to symbolise that undertone of hope, that new rhythm of optimism, which had just been perceptible in her father's last year. It became loud and clear and even more emphatic as the Coronation drew near.

A long reign stretched before Queen Elizabeth II and there was an urgent hope that this would bring a new age of prosperity, of strength, of

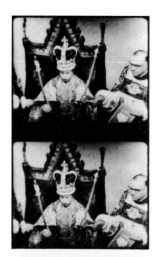

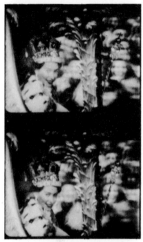

Top: The Queen crowned
Middle: The return to Buckingham Palace
Bottom: On the Balcony

confidence, a renewed greatness for Britain. And nothing could have been more auspicious than the fact that the news that Everest had been climbed was learnt by the crowds waiting in the rain for the Coronation procession. It had defeated men of skill and gallantry for decades.

The Coronation is the greatest of royal rituals; through its complex symbols it acknowledges the past, but also confirms the present moment in time, and pledges the future. The historic past stretches back into the mists of Scottish antiquity through the Stone of Destiny, encased in the chair made for it by Edward I after he had filched the Stone from the Scots. There are other relics from the medieval past too – the ruby that belonged to the Black Prince set in the Imperial Crown, the golden spoon and ampula used in the Anointing which may have been a part of King John's regalia. There are reminders of the Tudors in the huge pearls of Elizabeth I which had been inserted in the Imperial Crown. The Crown of St Edward with which all Kings and Queens are crowned was made for Charles II as the old crown had been broken up by the Republicans, but it is believed that some of the gold was re-used. However, neither the symbolism nor the regalia are entirely rooted in the past. Some changes are made in almost every reign. The Queen's dress was not only embroidered with the shamrock, the leek, the thistle and the rose – the symbols of the United Kingdom – but also with the wattle of Australia, the maple of Canada, the lotus of Ceylon and all the rest of the emblems of the Commonwealth. This, of course, was a decision of the Queen herself. She, too, decided on the reintroduction into the ritual of the gold armills or bracelets. These are a sacred as well as a royal emblem – they had been used to pledge the peace between King Alfred and the Danes a thousand years before – and they had last been used at the Coronation of Charles II. At the Queen's Coronation they were a gift from the United Kingdom and the principal Dominions; they represented 'peace and security', hopes that were in everyone's heart.

The future was present, too, not only in the pledges which the Queen made to the nation and the Commonwealth, but also in the decision which the Queen herself had taken – that the ceremony in all its elaborate and intimate detail should be televised. By that decision, instead of being witnessed by a few hundred fortunate people in the Abbey, the Anointing and Crowning were watched by millions. It was a bold and imaginative gesture for so young a monarch and a most decisive one. And yet it was within royal tradition. Monarchs were always shown to their people; indeed, the acclamation of the people was an integral part of ancient English Coronations and was certainly used at the time of the Conquest in 1066 by William I. It was called 'the recognition'. Partly a

The Queen arriving at Westminster Abbey for her Coronation, 2 June 1953

relic of the old Nordic form of the election to Kingship, it was also intended that the King should be seen and recognised. For the same reason the Norman Kings held courts in various parts of their kingdom – so that they could be seen and known. For time immemorial the monarchs of England had been concerned to spread their image. Coinage had been the first way of doing so; the slow, stately royal progress was another. The advent of the printing press brought a new means of disseminating the royal image, and so did the invention of the postage stamp which made their faces familiar in the remote corners of their dominions. Queen Victoria and Prince Albert were quick to realise the value and power of photography in its very early days. The film had scarcely been invented before it was being tentatively used at Balmoral and exploited for the great rituals of state – the Diamond Jubilee, the funeral of Queen Victoria. Wherever there had been a new technological achievement in communications, the Royal Family were often there among the forerunners in its use. During the twenties and early thirties, wireless sets had ceased to be the playthings of amateur enthusiasts sitting around a crystal set in headphones and became a feature of ordinary homes. King George V, a cautious man not given to innovation, had realised the immense value of radio and had initiated the Christmas Day message which had reached millions of his subjects throughout the world. Indeed the Queen herself had been initiated into the use of the wireless at the tender age of fourteen. On 13 October 1940, during the grimmest days of the war, she had broadcast to the children, many of them evacuated from their homes. She was to continue her father's and grandfather's practice of broadcasting on Christmas Day. Nevertheless the decision to televise the most intimate parts of the ritual of Coronation was a bold one and brilliantly successful. Richard Dimbleby had the right voice and manner – smooth, not unctuous: reverential without sycophancy. And millions of people sat enjoying in their parlours what previously had been a preserve of the aristocracy and the men and women of pomp and power.

It was to prove the beginning of more increasing visibility both for the monarchy and for the royal collections.

Royal travel to all parts of Britain by sea, rail and air is now an accepted and constant fact of life of the twentieth-century monarchy, but it was not always so. George IV's visits to Scotland and Ireland were the first which had been made by a reigning monarch since the time of the Stuarts. Above: 'Embarkation of George IV from Greenwich for Scotland August 1822' by Robert Havell

Below: King Edward VII's bedroom on the Royal Train, made for him in 1903. Still in use in 1939 and fitted with a scrambler telephone, this train was the base for King George VI's and Queen Elizabeth's visits to all parts of the kingdom during the early bombing raids of the 1939–1945 war

H.M.Y. 'Britannia', first used in 1954, has many reminders on board of earlier royal yachts. This binnacle (left) comes from the 'Royal George', George IV's yacht, and is not only a tribute to the nautical arts of the early nineteenth century but, with its ornate carving and gilding, typifies the lavish care and fine craftsmanship expended on all the possessions of George IV

One of the most interesting collections in the Royal Library is the prints, photographs and watercolours compiled for Queen Victoria recording every aspect of her homes and palaces, and the life lived in them. Her two royal yachts, both named 'Victoria and Albert', have a special series of their own. 'Prince Albert's Study' (middle left) and 'The Sitting Room' (opposite bottom), two watercolours painted on board the Queen's second yacht in 1864 by A. E. Penley, form not only part of the record of Prince Albert's rooms and possessions undertaken for his grieving widow, but also are a tribute to the care and precise thought which he had himself put into the planning and furnishing of their yacht. His gimbal table, which will stay level in the worst of storms, and which can be seen in his study, now stands in the Drawing Room of 'Britannia' (right). This room, designed by Sir Hugh Casson for the entertainment of large numbers of guests during state visits, makes an interesting contrast with the relaxed intimacy of the earlier 'Sitting-Room', obviously designed for family pursuits and conversation.
Below: Prince Philip's Study on board 'Britannia'

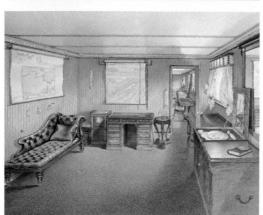

Far left: A Victorian naval review at Portsmouth: 'Queen Victoria visiting the Albion off Spithead, 21st June 1845' by John C. Schetky – watercolour (Royal Library)

CHAPTER TWO

THE WORLD ENCOMPASSED

Queen Elizabeth is the most travelled monarch the world has ever known. She has encircled the globe several times and visited the most remote parts of the Commonwealth. She has travelled in the British Isles just as extensively. In consequence she has been seen by millions of people in the flesh and by tens of millions of people through film and television, for these journeys arouse great popular interest. Never has the monarchy been so visible. Royal travel, however, is a most ancient tradition and an activity that has responded over the centuries to the developing needs and desires of the people. The monarchy, too, has always been quick to use developments in the technology of travel, from the carriage to Concorde.

In the early middle ages, the court was constantly on the move, even in peacetime: Westminster to Winchester; Winchester to Gloucester or Worcester; Worcester to a midland city, Northampton or Leicester. Sometimes the medieval kings would venture further North to Chester

Top: HRH The Duke of Edinburgh: 'Malay Village', one of many oil paintings made during his world tour in 1956–7

Bottom: Edward Seago: 'Race Meeting in the Chatham Islands' (oil, Windsor Castle)

or York. And, as they possessed Normandy and, later, Aquitaine and Gascony, they were frequently crossing the Channel and travelling through France, holding their courts and showing themselves to their French vassals.

There were several important reasons for this travel centuries ago. One was for the king to dispense justice in his court, and also to declare the law: his presence made the levying of taxes easier and his Exchequer travelled with him. His court was large and far too great a burden on the suppliers of food and fodder of any town, even London, for too long – so he had to move. Also he needed to show himself for more complex reasons – to display his strength, his glory, his kingship, his absolute difference from other men of his realm, no matter how powerful. A weak king might fail to do this, but strong kings did and it was they, not the weak ones, that kept the peace. Only a king could wear a crown; only a king could place the crown on his own head, after the coronation. Often the king wore his crown as he journeyed about his kingdoms in order to impress his subjects with his 'majesty' or his 'grace', words often used for a sovereign. Sometimes on these journeys the king would display his semi-magical powers by touching men, women or children for what was called 'The King's Evil' or scrofula, for his royal touch was thought to heal. Some of the sovereign's travels developed into specific royal rituals: in later times the king sat in solemn state with his nobles in the Great Council in Parliament which took place all over the land, not merely at Westminster; on the Thursday before Easter the king gave Maundy money to old men and women at one of the great churches or abbeys; and there were also the ritual crownings in great cathedrals. It was all a part of the magic and mystery of kingship.

As century followed century the practical aspects of the monarch's travels diminished: his courts of justice became permanently settled at his palace of Westminster; so did his Exchequer. The great civil wars in the fifteenth century did not permit much travelling except for the needs of war, but the Tudors revived the practice, particularly Queen Elizabeth I whose Court liked to escape the threat of plague that sometimes accompanied the heats of summer in London. Also the courts fouled up the palaces after a month or so and royal progresses gave welcome relief. The Queen also knew the value of her stately progress with her gentlemen courtiers – the long vivid procession of men at arms, noblemen with their retinues and she herself sitting like an icon on her famous litter. The majesty of monarchy was truly displayed. Her practice was followed in a more haphazard fashion by James I, hardly at all by Charles I, and Charles II preferred sauntering in St James's Park to making stately visits through the provinces. His people did, however, get a glimpse of him from time to time at the theatre or on the way to Newmarket, maybe, or to Winchester which he liked. He never travelled to display the majesty and mysticism of monarchy – his subjects saw him as it were incidentally. That was to be true of the monarchy for a long time. The Hanoverians might be seen on their way to Harwich when going to Hanover, or at formal visits to the universities, or on the way to race-meetings, and certainly once a year driving from Windsor to Ascot, a royal ritual which Queen Anne started. George III travelled rather more. His health was problematic and he went to Cheltenham Spa or Weymouth where he was loudly cheered by his subjects. He also began to develop novel methods of bringing the monarchy into contact with his subjects. For example, he paid a formal visit to Whitbread's Brewery, showing a fascinated interest in the latest technology, and also the Worcester China factory and a carpet manufacturer. He also, when at Cheltenham, went to the Three Choirs Festival which is, I believe, the first time a British monarch had attended a musical event outside the capital or the universities. Such visits, of course, almost dispensed with ritual (not quite, because there were the formal greetings; fanfares of trumpets and the like), but such visits were much more personal than the monarchy had ever undertaken before.

The monarch who really created the modern 'progress' was George IV, who had a considerable streak of theatricality in his make-up. From the days he was a child he loved dressing up, and he did it with immense panache combined with courtesy and charm. So he made very carefully planned state visits to Ireland and Scotland. In Edinburgh he had a very great success, appearing in the Royal tartan, emphasising that he was King of Scotland, the first reigning monarch since Charles II to set foot in Scotland, and the first king since William III to visit Ireland. He was immensely affable, meeting hundreds of people and setting a style for the future. It may, of course, all have come to nothing but for the development of the railway which made the travel of monarchs so much quicker and so much easier to plan carefully and accurately. Queen Victoria and her husband accepted more and more engagements to visit factories, to open important buildings, indeed to take a much greater part in the formal life of the nation whether it was in Liverpool, Newcastle, Plymouth or London. Royal trains were built to get them there in comfort; and royal yachts were constructed (George IV had one too) to take them to Ireland or overseas.

The death of Prince Albert made Queen Victoria very reluctant to appear in public and again this aspect of monarchy might easily have

Queen Victoria and Prince Albert welcoming Louis Philippe, the King of the French, and his Queen in 1843

been jeopardised but for her son, the Prince of Wales. Fortunately he adored movement. He was as naturally peripatetic as a Greek philosopher and, like most Greek philosophers, he could turn an elegant sentence in a trice. He was probably the best public speaker the Royal Family has ever produced – gracious, witty, elegant, brief. Hence he was greatly in demand, partly because of his mother's seclusion, and partly because he filled this role so brilliantly – looking every inch a monarch and discharging his duties with éclat.

Royal travel was developed in other ways by Edward VII, both as Prince of Wales and as King. State visits were rare under the Hanoverians, and indeed under all previous dynasties, relations between monarchs being left to ambassadors except for very special and unusual meetings like that between Henry VIII and Francis I at the Field of the Cloth of Gold. In all of Queen Elizabeth I's long reign, she never met another ruling monarch face to face. In 1735 the Duke of Lorraine, the sovereign of an independent duchy and the father-in-law of Louis XV of France, paid a visit to England but it was arranged very much on an *ad hoc* basis – the Duke being packed off to stay with Sir Robert Walpole at Houghton after a day or two at Court. From time to time there were similar semi-private visits. Queen Victoria and Prince Albert created a somewhat different convention. They invited the King of the French, Louis Philippe, to stay, entertaining him and the Queen much more formally. After he had been overthrown, they extended a similar welcome to Napoleon III and the Empress Eugénie. They afterwards visited Paris, taking with them their eldest daughter and the Prince of Wales, who loved it all so much that he developed something of a passion for state visits. During his reign a ritual for state visits developed. They lasted usually two or three days – each monarch would ceremoniously entertain the other; formal calls would be made on a dowager empress or queen, if alive; at some point there would be the review and inspection of troops or navies; at the end of a visit an order might be conferred by the kings on each other, sometimes the honorary colonelcy of a regiment (greatly favoured as it gave the opportunity of dressing up in splendiferous regimentals). Then would come the final ceremonial bestowal of gifts which, by the time Edward VII came to the throne, had been reduced to a very precise hierocratic system. Orders, carefully graded according to rank, were given to the major members of the suite; salvers went to others, cufflinks for the humbler. Even these were graded: some bore the royal cypher, some did not; likewise the humblest gift of all, a wallet – senior servants received it with a cypher, the more lowly without. Such visits had become ritual spectacles which entranced the gaping crowds

A view from the other side. A photograph of a welcoming crowd in Canada, taken by Prince Philip in 1959

The 'Britannia' arriving in Sydney in 1970. The Royal Family (left) photographed in May 1954 with the crew of 'Britannia', and the yacht being refitted in dry dock in 1960 (right)

that lined the Mall or the Unter den Linden or the Nevsky Prospekt. As the President of the French Republic possessed neither a royal title nor a regiment, the processions down the Champs Elysées were more sombre but the French made up in sashes what they lost in regimentals.

Most of these state visits were European (though not entirely – the Shah of Persia visited Queen Victoria), and for this the King's yacht, the *Victoria and Albert*, which he had used a great deal as Prince of Wales, was ideal. Splendid for reviewing navies, it could also take any amount of royal baggage to Copenhagen or St Petersburg or Kiel; indeed state visits would have been unthinkable without the use of this splendid royal yacht. The cases of orders now displayed in the Private Chapel at Windsor are very largely the direct result of King Edward's state visits and the return visits of so many Emperors, Kings and Presidents. The King's brothers, too, collected a fine haul of orders from all over the globe. After the deaths of the Duke of Windsor and the late Duke of Gloucester most of these have been incorporated into the Royal Collection which is now the finest in the world. Edward VII made one other forward-looking step in the world of royal travel. As a young man, calling himself the Duke of Renfrew, but known by everyone to be the Prince of Wales, he visited Canada and the United States with extravagant success. The British monarchy had escaped from the confines of Europe.

His son, George V, ventured further not only as Prince of Wales but also as King. He was received as Emperor of India at a great Durbar held in Delhi in 1911. The Great War, the economic crisis of the early twenties and his own precarious health curtailed his travelling, much as he enjoyed it. The granting of dominion status to Australia, Canada, New Zealand and South Africa enlarged even further the nature of state visits, and presaged an even greater extension for the future, when in this reign Empire changed inexorably year by year into a vast Commonwealth of independent countries linked through the Crown.

George VI travelled less than his predecessors. He was able to make one visit to Canada and a shorter one to the United States but, short though it was, the effects were lasting. He and Queen Elizabeth became firm friends with the President and Mrs Roosevelt. Perhaps the ice was thoroughly broken when a butler skidded into the Presidential drawing-room on his backside spilling glasses and drinks right and left. In any case, both the Roosevelts, like the King and Queen, were very easy people to like and admire. Then came the war. Like his father, the King visited his troops on the battlefields but state visits were matters of the past. Certainly he saw many of his fellow sovereigns – most of them were

HRH The Prince of Wales with some of the eskimo sculptures he has himself acquired or been given on visits to Northern Canada. The musk-ox (top left) by Irene Neooktook was a gift to Prince Charles from Madame Leger, wife of the Governor General of Canada. 'Tossing the Blanket', a group presented to The Queen, now stands on a table at the head of the Ministers' Stairs in Buckingham Palace

Gifts from the Commonwealth are displayed or in use throughout the royal buildings, but all four on this page are from Buckingham Palace. Ivory carvings from India (right) and Ghana (below right). Below left, a carved wooden box, part of a Silver Jubilee gift from President Nyerere of Tanzania. A paper weight from the Bahamas with a model of Columbus's ship, the 'Santa-Maria', and coins of his time around the base

Opposite: At the Commonwealth Institute, Kensington, children learn about the many different peoples and ways of life in the Commonwealth by handling gifts presented on Royal Tours which are on loan to the Institute

Below right: A girl in the class wearing a parka from the Canadian arctic, with a doll presented to The Queen tucked into the hood in the place of a baby

Left: One of the portable and folding spinning wheels invented by Mahatma Gandhi. His wedding gift to The Queen had been a piece of cloth of his own weaving

At Sandringham there is a Museum which includes many gifts from the United Kingdom and Royal Tours. This sculpture, 'The Two Champs' by Harry Jackson, was a gift to The Queen from President Ford of the United States of America.
Below: A Silver Jubilee gift from the Bahamas which hangs beside the swimming pool in the Orangery at Windsor Castle

on the run from Hitler and needed help, which they promptly obtained from the King and Queen who were very generous.

After the war, royal travel could be undertaken again but naturally England came first. Visits had been made during the war – to bombed-out Coventry for instance – but they had been few and scant, for the King's place was in London. Now it was time to travel the land again, to hearten and encourage and thank the people for what they had endured with such fortitude. This done, the King planned to visit all the major dominions of the Commonwealth except India, still split and full of religious strife in spite of the efforts of Lord Mountbatten. He did get as far as South Africa; but illness led to the cancellation of other visits to Australia and New Zealand. There was, therefore, a considerable backlog of travel awaiting the young Queen as soon as her Coronation was over. Sir Winston Churchill thought that she should encompass the world like Drake (the concept of a new Elizabethan age was very much to the fore in those heady days), the first reigning monarch to do so. It also meant that she could undertake the journeys postponed by her father's illness and add a number of other parts of the Commonwealth for good measure.

She set off by air, her eyes brilliant with tears as she waved goodbye for she was to be parted from her son and daughter for many, many months. Bermuda, the charming, anachronistic island, was the first stop: after Britain it possessed the oldest Parliament in the Commonwealth and of course the Queen visited it. Then she went on to the Caribbean, stopping in Jamaica, a country nearer to the problems and troubles that an ardent desire for independence was bound to bring. There she joined the *Gothic*, a small passenger liner of the Shaw Savill line which had been converted for her use, principally by equipping it with the most up-to-date communications system which kept the Queen in daily touch with her government and her family.

The *Gothic* steamed through the Panama Canal and headed west across the Pacific. She stopped at Tonga, whose gigantic Queen Salote, well over six feet tall and magnificently proportioned, had been so wildly cheered in the Coronation procession, sitting bolt upright in her open carriage in the driving rain and icy wind, radiant with delight. She had taken a London taxi-cab back with her and now met the Queen in it at the quayside. After Tonga came Fiji, an exceptionally loyal colony; now that it is independent, Her Majesty is the Queen of Fiji. The islanders had never expected a royal visit and they were wild with delight – and, like so many far outposts of the Commonwealth, what they expected to be a once and for all time proved not to be true. The Queen has been to Fiji three times in the first twenty-five years of her reign.

Christmas was spent in New Zealand – surprisingly enough Queen Elizabeth II was the first British monarch to set foot on its shores, but of course she visited as Queen of New Zealand. It was as Queen of Australia that she landed in Sydney for an exceptionally heavy programme over the ensuing two months. As Queen of the country she opened the Australian Parliament and, to give the occasion especial emphasis, she wore her Coronation dress. She carried out an extremely exhausting programme, travelling 10,000 miles by plane, 2500 by rail and 900 by car, listened to 200 speeches, and made 102 herself. Others might falter, even wilt, the Queen never did. For a very young monarch it must have been a gruelling ordeal but she turned it into a triumph. Nevertheless it was a relief to board the *Gothic* again and steam off towards Ceylon and enjoy the winter sunshine of the tropics. A quick stop was made at the Cocos-Keeling islands, a tiny copra-producing dependency in the wastes of the Indian Ocean, a coral reef island which gave enough privacy for picnics and swimming before the hard work started up again in Ceylon and Uganda (to complete the tour broken by the King's death). At long last the royal party reached Tobruk to rejoin her children who were staying with their uncle, Lord Mountbatten, who, as Commander-in-Chief of the Mediterranean fleet, was based at Malta.

Waiting at Tobruk was the most important addition to be made to the royal buildings and collections in this reign – the yacht *Britannia*. This had been laid down in George VI's reign but it was not ready by the time that the Queen had started on her world tour. Now it was completely fitted out, the crew trained, and all was ready. Even in 1954, the Mediterranean fleet was not unimpressive and the Queen reviewed it, the first royal occasion for the yacht. Lord Mountbatten, with his accustomed panache, led the fleet with such verve and speed, and so close to *Britannia*, that the Queen was splashed by the spray. After this splendid baptism the *Britannia* made its first royal cruise. There was a brief stop in Gibraltar; then came the dreaded Bay of Biscay and the rough Channel, neither of which the Queen enjoyed for she is not the best of sailors. The yacht at that time lacked stabilisers and rolled impressively. And so to the Thames and quiet waters again. The yacht steamed right up the river, under Tower Bridge, to the Pool of London and the waiting tens of thousands, including the Prime Minister, Sir Winston Churchill, and the entire Cabinet.

It must have been, in spite of the years of preparation, very daunting for the Queen to have Sir Winston Churchill as her first Prime Minister, yet it was also a marvellous link with the past and her own ancestry, for Churchill could recall the great Diamond Jubilee of Queen Victoria. He

The Queen on her tour of India in 1961, seen here with the Maharajah of Jaipur

had been a friend of her great-grandfather and grandfather. He had played an active part in the Boer War and a very great part in the two World Wars. He had met Gladstone and almost every great man of every nation in the world. Since his day Prime Ministers have come and gone – seven of them – and the Queen herself has met the heads of almost all countries in the world – and visited pretty well everywhere in the free world, for that first royal tour was to set the pattern for the future.

Every year, except in 1960 when Prince Andrew was born, the Queen has made a royal visit; even in the year that Prince Edward was born, 1964, she kept an engagement to go to Canada. There is scarcely an island group in the Commonwealth that she has not visited – all the Caribbean and most of the Pacific islands, and indeed some tiny and private ones such as West Plana Cay. The one major group, still a part of the Empire, which she has not visited is the Falkland Islands but that is almost certainly due to diplomatic reasons – it might be considered an inflammatory gesture towards Argentina, another of the countries she has not visited. And Prince Philip has travelled even further, visiting the Antarctic and the remoter, tinier dependencies such as Tristan da Cunha, Ascension Island, St Helena and Pitcairn. No monarch or consort has ever travelled so far or so frequently.

Although there are moments of peace and rest on many of these visits, they are all strenuous and would be impossible without the amenities provided by the royal cars, the royal trains, the Queen's flight and, above all, the royal yacht.

Royal yachts have existed since the days of Charles II, who had a passion for the sea. He raced against his brother on the Thames and in the Solent, trying out the new fast rigging, first invented by the Dutch. Indeed English yachts were so good that he made a present of one to the King of France, Louis XIV. George IV had his own yacht, *The Royal George*, which bore him through the tumultuous seas on his way back from his state visit to Ireland. The first of Queen Victoria's yachts, *The Victoria and Albert*, which combined steam and sail, was so fast that it outdistanced the French destroyer sent for its escort. Indeed there was a tradition, centuries old, that the royal yacht should embody the latest technology in the design of ships. The *Britannia* lived up to the tradition. It looked like a sleek, comfortable, small liner, but in fact it could be transformed quickly and efficiently into a small hospital ship – with operating theatres, a variety of wards, and all the special services that such a ship requires. It was also, of course, a small floating palace – a small state banquet can be held in it: the dining-room at its fullest extension can serve seventy-two people. In remote islands or in some countries where neither the embassy nor the local hotels could properly accommodate the Royal Family, the *Britannia* was essential. Without it the monarchy could never have travelled in the way that it has, nor entertained abroad in the way that it should. It was as essential to the Head of the Commonwealth as Buckingham Palace is to the Queen of England.

Like all other royal palaces, the *Britannia* is full of mementoes of the past. The oldest is the Lord High Admiral's verge which was made for Charles II's brother, James, Duke of York, in 1660 for use on state occasions. The Queen assumed the title of Lord High Admiral in 1964 and the verge was given to her to mark the occasion by the Lords Commissioners of the Admiralty. It is used once a year at the Lord High Admiral's divisions at Dartmouth, at the naval cadets' passing out parade, and in 1980 the Queen was present as Prince Andrew was one of the successful midshipmen. At the Jubilee Review of the Fleet at Spithead it was carried before the Queen at the dinner on the *Ark Royal*. There is no relic from the eighteenth century but the ornate binnacle on the Verandah Deck was a part of the equipment of *The Royal George*. There are, too, as there should be, splendid mementoes of Trafalgar – two large silver-gilt vases, one given to Nelson, the other to Admiral Collingwood who succeeded him as Commander of the Fleet.

But most of the historic features came from the three royal yachts, all called *Victoria and Albert*, which spanned not only Queen Victoria's reign but those of Edward VII and George V; indeed *Victoria and Albert III* was not broken up until 1955. One of the most impressive is the gimbal table designed by Prince Albert: the top adjusts to the motion of the vessel and so keeps all steady.

Sir Hugh Casson was responsible for the light and pleasing decoration of the staterooms and he managed to incorporate a considerable amount of furniture from earlier yachts: the tables in the Dining Room are from *Victoria and Albert III*, so is the mahogany bookcase in the Anteroom and all of the older furniture there. As a memento of the first voyage round the world the Queen has kept a settee and armchair from her Sitting-Room on the *Gothic* as well as the light brackets painted in old silver. On the wall of the Anteroom is a small tattered white ensign, a sad reminder of great bravery and endurance. It was flown by Captain Scott on his sledge as he made his way to the South Pole. It was recovered when his body was found in 1912 and given the next year by Commander Evans to King George V.

Along with the old there is much that is new. There are paintings, not great works of art but very nostalgic mementoes of important events in the *Britannia*'s life – one of the Queen arriving in the Port of London after the tour of 1954, one of Edward Seago's paintings of *Britannia*'s visit to the Antarctic, and many photographs of those who have commanded her. But everywhere there are mementoes of the *Britannia*'s voyages – literally scores of them, many of them from the Pacific Islands including an ike and porai from Tonga in 1970. The ike is a mallet used by Tongan women and the porai is a man's close-quarters fighting club. The Pitcairn Islanders who were visited in 1971 carved a shark in driftwood and all the adult islanders signed their name on the back. But not all the mementoes are ethnic objects from remote islands: the Swedish Navy presented an antique sword of 1786 when the Queen visited Sweden on a state visit in 1956. The most recent addition to the furnishings are two beautiful silk Persian rugs, one given by the Sheik of Bahrain and the other by the Emir of Abu Dhabi during the Queen's tour of the Gulf States in 1979.

However, neither the furnishings nor the decorations, fascinating as they are, are the really impressive feature of the *Britannia*. What impresses most is the size, made to seem even greater than it is by the open nature of the royal apartments (which derives from the yacht's dual function, for these sweeping rooms can be changed quickly into wards for a hospital ship).

The *Britannia* is a large yacht – 463 feet long, 55 feet wide and displacing 5000 tons. Painted in royal blue above and red below, a golden band circles the boat below the upper deck; the royal coat of arms is on the bow; the royal cypher on the stern; the berthing ropes are blue, specially made for the yacht. No one could deny her beauty or fail to appreciate her royal quality. And she is manned by an expert crew, half of whom spend all their service lives with her, the other half recruited for two years of service. Commanded by an admiral (Hugh Janion in 1980), there are twenty-one officers and 256 men under his command. The men, too, dress with a difference: they wear their jumpers tucked into their trousers, which are finished off with a black silk bow at the back. In addition to the crew a Royal Yacht band from the Royal Marines is embarked for major overseas tours – twenty-six musicians under the command of Captain Hoskins.

But the *Britannia* is used and used heavily. Already she has sailed over 600,000 miles as well as taking part in eight major and six minor naval exercises in her secondary role. During the Jubilee year the Royal Yacht steamed over 43,000 miles, circumnavigating England and Scotland in order to take the Queen to the major ports of the realm. Never a year goes by without the *Britannia* spending many months at sea and crossing at least one of the major oceans of the world.

'Britannia' becomes a travelling palace, a place for official entertaining. Here the Queen welcomes President Kekkonen on board during a visit to Finland in 1976

The Queen in New Zealand. Prince Charles watches as a presentation is made. The kiwi feather cloak the Queen is wearing was presented to her on her first visit to New Zealand after her Coronation in 1953

It is a floating palace, equipped like one, maintained like one, and it works like one. As with all other palaces it discharges several functions: it does not merely carry the Royal Family to remoter places of the Commonwealth; it is used to create amity not only between members of the Commonwealth but also amongst our allies and, in a quiet way too, it is used to promote British interests. In 1975, during a Caribbean tour, ninety Mexican and British businessmen were given a day's cruise in the Bay of Mexico. During the visit to Brazil, over 200 were entertained for a buffet luncheon. The Bicentenary visit to America in 1976 was a staggering success, not the least being the treat given to 100 businessmen from New York who were taken for a day's sail.

Of course, there are harsh critics of the *Britannia*. Mr William Hamilton regards it as a monstrous waste of public money. After all there are critics of the monarchy – there always have been, and frequently very much more bitter and savage than Mr Hamilton. But the monarchy has always cultivated, at least since Charles II's day, a robust relationship with its people. Monarchs are used to criticism. Over the centuries, they have usually been found wanting by some of their subjects. Charles I was too arrogant; Charles II too lazy; James II too obstinate; William III too Dutch; Queen Anne too stupid; George I too German; George II too henpecked; George III too mean; George IV too extravagant; William IV too convivial; Queen Victoria too remote; Edward VII too affable; George V too philistine – indeed, it has been impossible for any of them to satisfy everybody all of the time. This they know and for generations they have been amused by the antics of their critics. George II put up with obscene caricatures that make any of the grotesque statements of *Private Eye* look like required reading for a very strict convent for girls. George III and George IV were criticised in cartoons with a savagery that still, at times, makes one blush to look at them, but George IV made a huge collection of them to amuse himself and his guests. Indeed, most monarchs have collected cartoons – friendly or bitter – and both Prince Philip and the Prince of Wales possess (and display) a very rich collection of cartoons about themselves. Prince Philip has a whole lobby full of them just outside his sitting-room at Sandringham. By the standards of other reigns, the cartoons and criticisms of the present Royal Family are friendly, amusing and only occasionally in thoroughly bad taste; and rarely, if ever, savage. Of course the *Britannia* is expensive; so is Buckingham Palace – and the functions of the monarchy would be impossible to discharge without either. And by the standards of the cost of other Heads of State, Britain and the Commonwealth get off very lightly indeed.

Sir Huw Wheldon, photographed at Sandringham during the making of 'Royal Heritage' with some of Prince Philip's collection of cartoons showing the Royal Family

WELCOME HOME

BUT WHERE IN THE BLOODY ATTIC?

BLOODY PHOTOGRAPHERS

Cartoons from Prince Philip's collection show amused understanding of some of the problems of royalty, and often speculate about what the Royal Family really say about things in private

PHILIP! WHAT DOES O.H.M.S. MEAN?

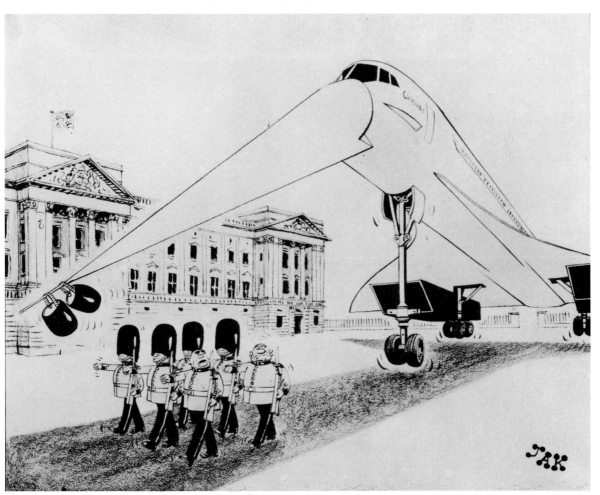

HE MUST THINK HE'S STILL IN HIS BLOODY HELICOPTER

The increased visibility of the monarchy through travel, through television, through the constant visits to and from other Heads of State has had an important effect on the nature of the royal collections themselves. Gift-exchange is almost as old as mankind. In the days of Homeric Greece, the *heroes* exchanged great cauldrons of bronze or rare objects of silver and gold. Unless the return gift was equally impressive the recipient of the original gift would be shamed. This exchange of gifts has persisted down the ages and in all parts of the world. When Lord MacCartney went on the first official diplomatic mission to China for George III, a great deal of discussion took place about the presents he should take with him which would particularly impress the Chinese Emperor. The usual type of gifts – objects of silver and gold or porcelain and silks – would have been totally inferior to what the Emperor enjoyed, so clocks, chronometers and scientific instruments were taken – alas with little avail. The Emperor had very complex instruments of his own, and he remained unimpressed.

Gift-exchange between Heads of State increased rather than waned during the nineteenth century, and the practice continues. In 1979, during her visit to the Gulf States, the Queen received remarkable presents in gold and silver and priceless jewels, for Arab sheiks have always been extremely lavish in their tradition of gift-exchange. Many of

The Queen in Hong Kong, 1975, painting the eye of the carnival dragon to bring it to life

these now adorn the drawing-room and dining-room of the *Britannia*. The Queen naturally did not attempt to outshine such beneficence but presented them all with large, inscribed silver salvers. Exchanges on state visits are always made and they are often neatly tailored to suit a particular Head of State. President Giscard d'Estaing is a very keen shot, so when he paid his state visit to Buckingham Palace he was presented with a retriever, trained by the Queen.

But it is not only gift-exchange between Heads of State that adds considerably to the collection. So do royal events – marriage, Coronation, the birth of children, those dramatic events of the Royal Family's life which are also public events for the nation and which create a surge of affection and loyalty that often finds expression by the sending of a gift – some magnificent, some modest, all moving. And, of course, on their travels the Queen and Prince Philip do not merely exchange gifts with Heads of State. Many people, many children, wish to present some token of affection: on one occasion a small girl gave her Mars bar to the Queen – probably, to her, very precious indeed. There was an even more embarrassing occasion when, in spite of the plea that no animals should be given, a small crocodile was presented to the Queen in West Africa in a biscuit tin. For the rest of the journey it travelled in Sir Martin Charteris's bath and ended up at the London Zoo. Most of such presents, however, are of an ethnic kind – tribal carvings, bead work, stone objects, textiles of all kinds, even boomerangs, shields and assagai find their way into the holds of *Britannia*. It is impossible for the Queen to house and display such an avalanche of gifts; indeed, her predecessors had the same problems.

There are some gifts, of course, of such outstanding beauty that they are kept. On her first visit to Australia in 1954 the Queen was given a brooch of very rare yellow diamonds in the form of a wattle, the national emblem of Australia, and now she always wears it on her visits there as Queen of Australia – a most appropriate gift that has become a regal symbol. Naturally such important gifts from the leading countries in the Commonwealth find a permanent niche in the collections. Some gifts fill a singularly appropriate place in royal palaces, but the Queen also has a discerning eye for the unexpected place. At the top of the Ministers' Stairs at Buckingham Palace is a very impressive group of eskimo art, given to her by the Canadian Government. It shows a circle of eskimos taking part in one of their traditional sports – tossing a man in a blanket. The group is full of vigour and movement. Some presents fit like a hand in a glove once the exact spot has been found. For the Jubilee in 1977 the Bahamas presented a signally beautiful collage of shells from its myriad beaches and coral reefs, that fitted perfectly into the Orangery, built by Wyatville, which runs under the North Terrace at Windsor, which has been converted for royal recreation – a polo practice net, ping-pong table, badminton court and, where the shells are most appropriate, a swimming pool. Few in the vast crowds that throng the North Terrace realise that below their feet is one of the few places where the Royal Family can relax and exercise in privacy.

Another present from Australia, also given in 1977 to mark the Jubilee, a young racehorse of that name conceived in that year, will fit as smoothly and, one hopes, as successfully into the royal stud as the Bahaman shells by the pool. Great skill is needed to fit many of these presents into an appropriate context. At first sight, some seem start-lingly incongruous – like the immensely high totem pole that now stands in Windsor Park. It came from Vancouver where it was carved by the Kwakiutl Indians. Vancouver weather – storm-ridden and often slashed by gales of rain – is sometimes experienced at Windsor and then the totem, looming in the wind-driven sky, seems as threatening, as magical as they do in Vancouver itself; and utterly at home.

Occasionally it is possible to display a whole group of presents together. In the corridor leading to her private apartments at Bucking-ham Palace the Queen has had constructed a beautiful display cabinet for glass. The background is grey-blue which gives a sharper definition to the glass and this, combined with strong lighting, makes a most dramatic decoration to the corridor. The glass itself is particularly fine. At the time of the Queen's marriage President and Mrs Truman gave 'a casket-shaped glass vase and cover of Steuben crystal, designed by the American sculptor, Sidney Waugh'. It is very beautifully engraved with the picture of a merry-go-round at an American country fair. The American Am-bassador and his wife chose the same sculptor for a set of twelve plates, also in Steuben glass, which are engraved with birds based on the wonderful prints of Audubon, the greatest of all painters of birds. There are other beautifully engraved pieces of glass by the great English engraver, Laurence Whistler. This display was only put together very recently and it incorporates also a particularly fine and unusual piece of glass, given to the Queen at her Jubilee in 1977. This is a goblet, attractively engraved in Hebrew lettering, that was given by the Association of Jewish Ex-servicemen and Women. It was a brilliant idea to bring these presents together and display them in this way.

But there are still many presents – valuable and important – that the royal collections cannot house, and so the British Museum, the National Maritime Museum, the Museum of Mankind take their pick and they go

Engraved glass from the Royal Collection.
Facing: Laurence Whistler: Glass vase engraved with English Landscapes. Presented to the Queen when she opened the new London Stock Exchange in 1972.
Overleaf: A Steuben crystal vase, and a crystal vase presented to the Queen and Prince Philip for their silver wedding anniversary in 1972 with an engraved view of the Glassaltshiel, Queen Victoria's small house beside Loch Muick on the Balmoral Estate

to them on a semi-permanent loan. This, too, is a well-established royal tradition. The British Museum has an outstanding pair of ivory Benin leopards which were loaned by Queen Victoria, and have been there ever since. Yet many small gifts remain, not important enough for the national museums. These are often fascinating small objects from the tiny islands and dependencies of the British Commonwealth or from East and West Africa or given, perhaps, by the indigenous peoples of Australia or New Zealand or Canada. These most appropriately go to the Commonwealth Institute where they are used in teaching – particularly the teaching of children who are fascinated by them.

This, too, is part of royal tradition. Recently children at the Institute were playing on drums from East Africa – the large one had been presented by Edward VII, the three small ones by Princess Margaret, for all members of the Royal Family make contributions to this scheme. The children love these objects which they can rapidly assimilate into their imaginations. There are models of outrigger canoes from the New Hebrides, a war canoe from the Solomons. One little girl enjoyed putting on the Eskimo dress made for the Queen and an Eskimo doll was put into the pocket at the back where normally the Eskimo baby would go – the girl was wild with delight; for one brief moment she was Queen, Eskimo, mother, all in one. Some teach tougher lessons. One of Mahatma Gandhi's patent collapsible spinning wheels (it folds very neatly into a portable box), which he invented in Jarvarla Jail in Poona, was given to the Queen when she visited his memorial in 1961. It is made to work for the children and is an easy introduction to a lesson about India, Gandhi, independence and the problems facing a vast peasant population. And so to the generosity of the giver is added the generosity of the Queen and the other members of the Royal Family. Such gifts could not be put to better use.

Some of the most touching gifts come from the people of the British Isles at great moments of the reign, and this was particularly true of the Jubilee celebrations in 1977 when rich and poor, the distinguished and the unknown, felt a need to express their loyalty and affection by sending a gift. Over a thousand gifts poured into the palace, from heads of government, from public and private bodies, from schools and associations of every kind, and from many individuals of all ages. Often they expressed the donors' own interests – the artists sent portraits and pictures, the singers records, the craftsmen and craftswomen examples of their art; some people with strong religious views sent bibles or books on religious topics; many small towns and villages proudly despatched histories of their communities; but many were simple, heartfelt presents

Vase of Steuben crystal designed by Sidney Waugh, a wedding present to the Queen and Prince Philip from President and Mrs Truman

– two handkerchiefs, a tablecloth, a tea-cosy, a lavender sachet. Some were the work of children whose imagination had been fired by the Jubilee. Not all came from the United Kingdom – all the countries of the Commonwealth sent gifts (many sent not one but several), and many individuals even in remote places expressed their loyalty in presents great and small. The Mayor of Paderborn, Germany, sent a medallion commemorating a thousand years of Paderborn; the Californian Historical Society sent a box of artefacts connected with Francis Drake; whilst Maître G. Salman sent a lace cloth from France. Indeed the display at St James's Palace filled the State Apartments. In this plethora of gifts were many of artistic importance and will find a permanent place in the collections. But in addition over 100,000 men, women and children, largely from the United Kingdom, felt impelled to write – often in verse – to the Queen on her Jubilee. Indeed loyalty and affection welled up to a most unprecedented degree.

In this reign Sir Hugh Casson, in addition to his impressive work on the *Britannia*, has been responsible, among many other projects, for the design and the interior decoration of some of the private apartments at Windsor. He has created, for example, the visitor's suite in Edward III's Tower at Windsor, which shows off to great advantage contemporary

Edward Ardizzone: 'Waiting in the X-ray Department'. One of the watercolours presented to the Queen by the Royal Academy on the occasion of her Jubilee

Waiting for an X ray

craftsmanship in furniture, textiles and glass. He was President of the Royal Academy in Jubilee year and he asked the artists of the Royal Academy to contribute a watercolour, drawing or print for presentation to the Queen. In the end there were three boxes of them. Sir Hugh presented a charming watercolour of Windsor Castle, Elizabeth Frink a powerful working drawing of a horse, the late Edward Ardizzone a vivid and ominous drawing 'Waiting in the X-ray Department'; Peter Blake, the best of the pop artists, gave an engaging study of 'Puck'. Some artists made their own presentations, and Graham Sutherland, whose work the Queen and the Duke of Edinburgh admired, sent a set of his latest series of lithographs – 'the Bees' – a series which, alas, was to be his last. (Unfortunately only the Queen Mother had been brave enough to be sketched by Sutherland, the greatest yet most candid portraitist of our time.)

Every year gifts flow in and many gifts are truly impressive. Some are made deliberately by their donors because they realise that the royal collections are more appropriate for their gifts than a national museum. Typical of this kind of gift is the marble group of Mrs Jordan and children, recently bequeathed to the Queen, or the service of early Worcester china (lily pattern) given for Queen Charlotte's Cottage in Kew Gardens (this was most appropriate because it is of the same date as the cottage and Worcester was also the one china factory to be visited by George III). Dr Hunter and his mother, Dr MacAlpine, who had devoted a great deal of their lives to studying George III's illnesses, presented their collection of medals, documents and mementoes relating to the King which have been added to the small museum of similar objects at the Dutch house in Kew.

This aspect of the growth of the royal collections is similar to what happens at a great museum which is constantly acquiring material by gifts and bequests. Naturally the Surveyors of the Royal Collection would not advise the acceptance of every object for permanent display and obviously they are guided by considerations of what is apposite and what fills a gap in what already exists. If an object had a proven association with the Royal Family and its ancestors, then the gift makes a strong claim; otherwise not.

Gifts come from a whole variety of sources and in bulk they are the most considerable addition to the Royal Collection but not the only one. From time to time objects and pictures are purchased, and also royal patronage of the arts still flourishes.

CHAPTER THREE

ACQUISITIONS

The world of art has been in a state of hyper-inflation since World War II. Before the crash in 1929, the heyday of Duveen and Berenson, wildly extravagant prices were paid by rich Americans such as Frick, Carnegie, Mellon and J. P. Morgan. Alas, such prices, even allowing for inflation, seem no longer excessive, indeed cheap. Nowadays American museums command even greater resources than the great American entrepreneurs and fine and rare pictures can fetch up to two million pounds. Even the great Impressionists and the Post-Impressionists can bring staggering sums – three quarters of a million pounds, often a quarter of a million for what might be described as a run-of-the-mill Cézanne or Renoir. These enormous prices, which are reflected, too, in other works of art, have had an effect, naturally enough, on the acquisition policy of the Royal Family.

Splendid as the Royal Collection of paintings is, there are still great gaps in it because, after the death of Prince Albert in 1861, no monarch

Sir Francis Chantrey: 'Mrs Jordan and Children'. Mrs Jordan was an actress and the mistress of the Duke of Clarence, later William IV

was particularly interested in painting and certainly not in any painting which deviated from the conventional standards of the Royal Academy. Edward VII and Queen Alexandra missed golden opportunity after golden opportunity to enrich the collection but the King's taste was limited. He liked to have paintings of his horses and he enjoyed the yachting pictures by de Martino, who painted with verve and skill. His other important additions were very few – a fine portrait called *Bianca*, painted by Lord Leighton whom he had met in Rome and who had given him a companion picture, and there are three by Gustave Doré at Sandringham which were purchased during his lifetime, one of which is of a most seductive nymph in high Victorian style. Queen Alexandra loved Fabergé and trinkets, not pictures. Indeed she preferred photography and watercolours to paintings. Edward VII's circle of friends did not consist of art lovers, apart from the Rothschilds and the Kassels, who were busy buying what the King clearly had in plenty – Old Masters. His other friends had art galleries of their own, full of Old Masters bought by their ancestors; indeed, some were longing to sell the occasional picture to the Americans so long as it could be done surreptitiously.

George V was less interested, if anything, than his father, although he liked Munnings. Queen Mary loved works of art, and certainly enjoyed looking at pictures, but unless they related directly to her ancestors she would not buy them. She was particularly interested in what she called 'the old Royal Family' – George III and Queen Charlotte and their immediate descendants; she missed important pictures in this field, but she may have felt that the austere times in which she lived did not warrant any large expenditure on portraits. It is strange, however, that she never bought a Sickert and that she was never painted by Sargent. What a marvellous subject she would have made for him! The only Sargents in the collection – the portraits of the Duke and Duchess of Connaught – came as gifts to George VI. Fortunately, Queen Elizabeth, the Queen Mother, before the immense leap in prices took place after the war, was able to repair some of these omissions by buying some fine English paintings as well as one or two Impressionists in the 1930s. These are, of course, Queen Elizabeth's own pictures: a corollary of the Royal Collection but not really a part of it; indeed they may never be.

There is now, indeed, no hope that the great gaps that exist in the Royal Collection of paintings can ever be filled. It is ironic that our Hanoverian monarchs are often despised for their philistine attitudes. The remark of George II that he did not 'like bainting and boetry' is often quoted to summarise their attitude but it is certainly not true. He, like his son and grandson, employed some of the leading British artists

Louis-Gabriel Blanchet: 'Prince Charles Edward Stuart'. This is one of the important portraits, illustrated on this and the following pages, which were acquired during the present reign and fill gaps in the history of the Collection. It was bought to hang in the Palace of Holyroodhouse, Edinburgh

Above: Samuel Cooper: Hugh May, Charles II's architect at Windsor. Left: Sir Godfrey Kneller: Henry Wise, gardener to William III and Mary II at Hampton Court and Kensington Palace. Below: Johann Zoffany: Portrait study – 'George III, Queen Charlotte and their family'. Right: Gerrit van Honthorst: 'The Children of the King and Queen of Bohemia'. (Detail) Princess Elizabeth as 'Diana', with Prince Rupert

of their day: the only outstanding neglect, ironically enough, was of Constable and Turner, and this was due to the greatest connoisseur of them all, George IV. The early monarchs of the twentieth century simply cannot compare with the Hanoverians – they were the least interested in paintings of any monarchs since the middle ages. To repair the gaps they unwittingly left would cost tens of millions of pounds by current prices and the funds are just not there and never will be.

And so the policy of acquisition has, of necessity, to be more modest in its aims. It has two principal features. One is to continue and extend what Queen Mary started: that is to acquire pictures and objects that relate directly to the history of the British monarchy or complement what is already in the collection and so give it added depth. The other is to acquire a small and personal collection of works by modern artists, either British or Commonwealth. Europe and America are ignored not because they are disliked but because the field would then be far too large.

The latter policy is more difficult than it may seem at first sight. Since World War II, and perhaps even before, modern art had entered a period of chronic anarchy, almost of self-destruction. There are more artists at work now than ever before but they are no longer, most of them, working within an accepted tradition. One folly has been to assume that anyone with technical excellence as a painter or sculptor should also be deeply original and creative. This has led to some of the wilder absurdities of modern art, as the technically proficient have striven to be original at any cost. So if you walk along the corridors of Buckingham Palace or Windsor you will not find a tastefully arranged heap of bricks trying to masquerade as a work of art. Nor if you are privileged to enter the private apartments of the Royal Family will you see a curiously shaped canvas painted entirely in black or blue or white leaning against the wall pretending to be a picture. The gardens at Balmoral, at Sandringham, or Windsor are not festooned with brightly painted, neatly welded girders. The huge, swinging mobiles of Calder are not to be found there. (Perhaps one may here regret one omission. The famous sculpture of 'King and Queen', one of Henry Moore's finest, would sit superbly on a rocky outcrop of the mountains about Balmoral.) Actually there is one admirable piece of modern sculpture on the East Terrace at Windsor. It is a fountain, designed as a tulip, and it is by His Royal Highness Prince Philip: it blends beautifully with the bronze figures by Le Sueur, cast for Charles I, which are themselves interspersed with the lead vases designed by Willem van Mieris, which represent the Seasons and were bought by George IV in 1825.

William Dobson: Charles, Prince of Wales, later Charles II (Detail). A portrait painted during the Civil War in 1644 at the Royalist army headquarters in Oxford. The armour he is wearing is now on display in The Armouries at The Tower of London

In such a plethora of schools from Minimalists to Abstract Expressionists there can be no safe guide. The only sensible policy, and the one which has been pursued, was to buy what one liked: to see as much as possible and then to choose. Fortunately the Queen and Prince Philip have a real and genuine interest in art. The Queen, after all, was brought up in an art-loving family, for which the acquisition of a Sisley or a Matthew Smith or a Lowry was an important event. And Prince Philip has considerable artistic talent. Whenever he can, he gets into his studio at Windsor and paints, mainly landscape and the life to be found in nature – birds are a favourite topic. His watercolours and oils attain a very high standard and one day may become a part of the Royal Collection itself like the architectural drawings of George III or Queen Victoria's enchanting watercolours.

One attitude towards acquisition was established by Queen Mary who brought an almost professional knowledge and enthusiasm to the royal collections. She knew them better, far better than most of the Surveyors of her time. Hence she was very conscious of where a gap might be filled and she was always on the alert when making one of her peregrinations amongst the antique shops and picture dealers. She had *trouvailles* great and small – a snuff box with the Prince Regent's profile in ivory but also, more importantly, a Lely that was finished by Benedetto Gennari of the Duke and Duchess of York with Princess Mary and Princess Anne. Fortunately scholarly investigation could pinpoint exactly when Gennari finished the picture in 1674; unfortunately Gennari's work was very coarse but the composition and some of the painting is by Lely. Queen Mary bought it at Sotheby's in 1933. A more charming picture was purchased the next year – a pastel of William, Duke of Gloucester, the brother of George III, which Horace Walpole described as 'exceedingly like'. Queen Mary knew that there was a miniature of this at Windsor so the original pastel added significantly to the collection. Earlier she had bought a Beechey and there were other significant purchases that gave added strength to the collection. This process was continued by George VI and Queen Elizabeth. Indeed it was Queen Elizabeth who purchased in April 1951 Bower's extremely moving picture of Charles I at his trial: one of the most haunting pictures in the Royal Collection.

Another valuable purchase was a splendidly detached bird's-eye view of Hampton Court in the reign of George I, which illustrates the important changes made by Henry Wise, Queen Anne's great gardener, to the setting of Hampton Court – a setting which still partly persists. At the time this picture was painted Hampton Court was enjoying a

Prince Philip: Vaduz Castle

renewed and vigorous life after a period of neglect. The Stuarts had used it hardly at all, whereas William and Mary had commissioned Wren to build new courts and new staterooms, and the early Hanoverians enjoyed Hampton Court as much as William and Mary had done. So this picture shows Hampton Court in full bloom, as it were: within thirty years this great palace had been deserted once more by the monarchy and this time finally. Indeed George III expressed the hope that it might have burnt down. And so this picture, not intrinsically perhaps of great aesthetic value, has very great importance for the history of the royal palaces. Its acquisition complemented a former purchase made in December 1947 by King George VI when he bought Kneller's portrait of Henry Wise, the gardener.

This type of acquisition has been developed and extended by the Queen. Her Surveyors are constantly on the alert for pictures of reasonable price that will add further depth to the collection, and they have been remarkably successful. Indeed, they have acquired some pictures of exceptional quality as well as being historically important. In 1955 the

Queen bought a Hogarth (and the Royal Collection was not rich in Hogarths) of George II and his family, an oil sketch painted in 1730–1. Although the heads are not painted from the life (indeed, they are just sketched in), the picture is an important one because of its history. There is an entry in the notebooks of George Vertue where Hogarth complains 'he had some time ago begun a picture of all the royal family in one peice by order the sketch being made'. However, much to Hogarth's chagrin, the picture had been stopped. The sketch remained in Hogarth's possession and Sir Oliver Millar was able to trace its descent through his executor, Samuel Ireland, to America, from where it was retrieved by the Queen. Again the importance of the picture gains immensely from its history which is so intimately bound up with the Royal Family. Hogarth was stopped by the intervention of his rival William Kent: artistic jealousy prevented a finished picture being painted, but the sketch remains.

Other purchases have helped to dispel legends. George I caused some surprise when he came to England by retaining the services of two Moslems whom he was said to have captured at the Siege of Vienna in 1683. This was in fact untrue: they were a present from a Polish nobleman. The imagination and pens of historians got to work on these 'arab' servants and they have acquired a somewhat sinister air. Actually they were not Arabs but Turks, and one, Mehemet, was highly educated and a complete gentleman who acted as personal secretary to George I. His portrait by Kneller was recently purchased and he appears dressed as an English gentleman with fine intelligent eyes and strong features.

Naturally the Hanoverians did not look with much favour on their Stuart cousins who, in the 1715 and 1745 rebellions, did their best to topple them from the throne. George IV, the forty-five long forgotten, was able to take a more relaxed view, and when Henry Cardinal York, the last of the Stuart line, fell on hard times, he paid him an annuity and when he died secured, after extraordinary vicissitudes, a vast mass of archives, now at Windsor. As a mark of gratitude for the annuity, the Cardinal bequeathed a few jewels to George IV, then Prince of Wales, including a ruby ring with a cross which had belonged to Charles I. It is now at Edinburgh with the Scottish regalia. Since that time, the Royal Family has acquired more and more Stuart relics, including particularly fine portraits of the Stuart princes by Blanchet, which are now at the Palace of Holyroodhouse.

In this way pictures are constantly being added to the Royal Collection, but before purchases of historical portraits are made the scholarship of the Surveyor of the Queen's Pictures, Sir Oliver Millar, is brought to bear on the purchase – its quality, its authenticity, the way it fits into the collection and the way it will enrich it. Pictures are not bought because they are 'nice' or catch the fancy. They are acquired with the same care and attention that a great gallery or museum would give to its acquisitions.

As with pictures, so with drawings – in many ways a task equally formidable. The royal collections contain a very remarkable number of drawings from the early Renaissance to modern times. There are thousands of sketches of royal persons and royal occasions, going back at least as far as Holbein, as well as a great number of Old Master drawings. Again, however, the collection is uneven: very rich in some aspects, weak in others. But because of the inflated prices in the art world, it is not possible to strengthen the Old Master drawings by expensive purchases; nor is it desirable because the individuality of the collection would be destroyed because it has been shaped by the varying tastes of the monarchs who assembled it. Purchases are largely confined to drawings and watercolours of royal personages or royal palaces.

Recently the contents of the studios of Sir James Gunn and Sir Gerald Kelly were sold. Gunn had painted the Royal Family and, indeed, had painted one of the most enchanting royal conversation pieces of this century: *King George VI and Queen Elizabeth with the two Princesses at tea in the Royal Lodge*, now in the National Portrait Gallery. Amongst the drawings from his studio, there were studies for this picture which were bought by Queen Elizabeth, the Queen Mother. A similar opportunity occurred in 1979 when the contents of Sir Gerald Kelly's studio were sold. Amongst them were studies of both George VI and Queen Elizabeth. These were acquired by the Queen and they make an admirable documentary comment on the state portraits by Kelly.

Purchases of drawings or watercolours dating from earlier centuries are for the most part confined to royal themes – portraits of former monarchs and their families, views of royal residences and estates, records of royal functions. Advice on historical purchases is given by the Curator of the Print Room in the Royal Library, Jane Roberts, who is in direct charge of the collection under the Royal Librarian.

Among recent acquisitions which the Queen was glad to secure are two remarkable coloured drawings of Windsor Castle by Paul Sandby, an artist who lived in Windsor Great Park in the second half of the eighteenth century and became a celebrated exponent of the peculiarly English discipline of painting in watercolours. George IV appreciated his talents and began to collect his drawings, particularly those which depicted Windsor and its environs. From time to time purchases of similar material have been made. In this century Sandby's reputation has steadily grown and his work is much sought after by collectors. One of these works, in watercolours, is a view of Windsor Castle from the north-east across the river Thames. The other, in gouache, depicts the South-east corner of the Castle from the Home Park.

Among the drawings and watercolours added to the collection for their historical interest are several of a relatively modest artistic standard. Such is a watercolour by W. I. Pocock of the fantastic castellated gothic palace at Kew that George III began to build but never finished. Apart from a single print this is the only representation of it in the collection. As the palace was demolished in the reign of his son it is of particular architectural and topographical interest. An acquisition of a different character is a drawing in gouache by Prince Augustus, later Duke of Sussex, one of the seven sons of King George III who survived infancy. It shows no great talent, but found its proper home in the set of works by the young children of that King which have been in the Royal Library since its foundation nearly 150 years ago.

Preparatory studies for royal portraits in preceding centuries are also acquired from time to time. One such is the design for the portrait of William IV, by Wilkie, in the uniform of the Grenadier Guards which now hangs in the Wellington Museum at Apsley House. A group of drawings by Benjamin West was purchased in 1980. These are studies for the portraits of George III's children, already in the Royal Collection.

The addition of this kind of material to the Royal Collection does more than serve the interests of its owner: its presence among related works in a collection which is easily accessible and whose contents are available to qualified researchers represents an important contribution to national scholarship.

Richard Parkes Bonington:
'A Coast Scene in Normandy'

Apart from the addition of pictures, drawings and prints of historical importance, the collection has been enriched by the Queen and Prince Philip's important collection of modern artists. The modern collection was started very early in the reign, for a time with the aid of a committee of experts: but Prince Philip has always pursued his own lines of interest. He was attracted by the vivid portraits of Feliks Topolski, who sketched the sitters in John Freeman's famous series of television interviews *Face to Face*. The Prince bought many of them. They are full of insight into the character of the sitter, as revealing indeed as the interviews themselves. There is a marvellously arrogant Edith Sitwell, an almost too avuncular J. B. Priestley and a brilliant Lord Hailsham, amongst others. They are extremely vivid images of the outstanding men and women of the 1940s and 1950s. They now hang in a corridor in the Private Apartments at

W. I. Pocock: 'Gothic Palace
at Kew'

Windsor. Because the Prince found these drawings so striking he commissioned Topolski to paint the Coronation Procession. This, again, was very much in the royal tradition for George IV had his procession painted in a huge book, one of the largest books ever made and opulent with gold leaf. Before this, there had been prints of the Hanoverian and Stuart Coronation Processions. Topolski's painting now takes up a very long wall in a corridor at Buckingham Palace. It is vivid, lively, somewhat jumbled in the Topolski manner. It is great fun picking out the faces of great contemporaries but it does miss somewhat the majesty and grandeur of the occasion. And in some mysterious way it is dominated by the figure of Winston Churchill. In 1953 his prestige was vast and all eyes watched him as he moved slowly up the aisle at Westminster Abbey on that June morning. With his years of experience and vast reputation he can only have been a daunting mentor in spite of the Queen's long years of training for her accession. Also Churchill possessed an almost baroque veneration for the throne which cannot have made for ease. So perhaps this dominating presence in the Coronation Procession is just.

There is no doubt of the regard that the Queen held for Sir Winston for she commissioned a magnificent head of him by Oscar Nemon for Windsor Castle. He is the only one of her Prime Ministers to be so honoured. Nevertheless the tradition is an old one. Queen Victoria had portraits of her favourites – Melbourne, Disraeli, Salisbury and others, but not Gladstone. (He is, however, to be found on a screen at Sandringham, in a collage of photographs made by Queen Alexandra when Princess of Wales.) Prince Philip also has, in his study at Buckingham Palace, a collection of other Prime Ministers and some of the leading politicians of the reign: small figurines of extreme realism that just border on caricatures. One or two – the Attlee, the Morrison, the Aneurin Bevan, are admirable in their accuracy and insight.

However, there remained the question of which paintings to collect. Considering the anarchic state of modern art the only viable policy was to go for what one liked and leave the future to judge the quality of one's taste. Any collection of modern art is easy to criticise, and the collection made in this reign can certainly be criticised – abstract art is absent; there is no David Hockney yet, no Francis Bacon, no sculpture by Henry Moore. Most of us would find it difficult to live with Francis Bacon's tortured studies of agonised flesh, great though they may be; and at times Moore is repetitive, solemn, almost tedious with gravitas, so one can see the argument against buying them. Yet it is a pity that one or two of his monumental sculptures are not scattered about the royal gardens and parks. As for Hockney, one only hopes that sooner or later a drawing

Sir James Gunn: State Portrait of The Queen in her Coronation Robes (Detail)

Sir Gerald Kelly: Sketch for a portrait of Queen Elizabeth (The Queen Mother)

Michael Noakes: HM The Queen
Pietro Annigoni: HRH The Duke of Edinburgh
Sir James Gunn: Sketch of The Duke of Windsor
in Garter Robes

Feliks Topolski: Two of the paintings of the Coronation commissioned by Prince Philip. Top: In the Abbey. Prince Philip's procession with foreign and colonial rulers. Below: The Queen's Procession through the streets with the massed bands of footguards

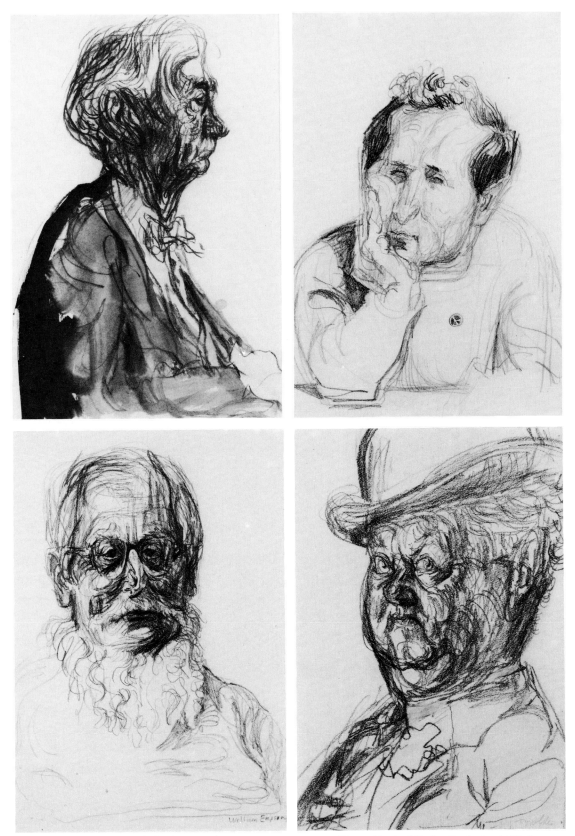

Feliks Topolski: Drawings, made for the BBC television interview programme 'Face to Face', of Herbert Read, Arnold Wesker, William Empson, and Evelyn Waugh

Feliks Topolski: Further 'Face to Face' drawings. W. H. Auden, and (facing)
Ivy Compton-Burnett, Compton Mackenzie, Cecil Day-Lewis, and Stephen Spender

Cecil Day Lewis

Stephen Spender

or two will slip in, before his prices soar out of reach.

The collection of modern artists, in spite of some obvious lacunae, is impressive – certainly the most impressive addition to pictures since Prince Albert died. Edward Seago, who painted seascapes and estuaries under the wide Norfolk skies so well, is heavily represented with a remarkable series on the Antarctic. Sea pictures naturally attracted Prince Philip, and a Montagu Dawson schooner sails majestically across the windswept ocean in his study at Buckingham Palace.

One of the most interesting parts of the modern collection is a group of Australian painters. Australia, more than any other Commonwealth country, has produced over the last fifty years painters of great capability and distinction, and the royal collections have some particularly fine examples. There is a splendid Sidney Nolan, *The Watering Hole*, one of the many of his pictures that were inspired by the drought in the outback. There are other Nolans, a couple of outstanding Dobells, a Drysdale of distinction, and a fascinating group of Aboriginal art with its haunting and evocative patterns. Apart from the Australian group, most of the pictures are in the mainstream of British art – several very good Nashes, an outstanding Lowry, *The Carriage*, and fine examples of Ivon Hitchens, Darwin, Rowntree, Armstrong, de Grey, Davie and one or two excellent watercolour sketches by the late Graham Sutherland as well as the magnificent cartoon of the tapestry that hangs in the new Cathedral at Coventry. Indeed it could be argued that the Sutherlands are the finest of the modern collections: for the Jubilee he himself added his remarkable series of lithographs called *The Bees*. Prince Philip's great interest both in observing and painting natural history subjects has led him to assemble an impressive collection of drawings and watercolours, including some very fine ones indeed by Janet Marsh.

It is impossible to leave the story of the acquisition of paintings without saying far more of the patronage of Edward Seago that rapidly ripened into friendship with three generations of the Royal Family. Seago had acquired a huge popular reputation in the years immediately after the war – queues formed outside Colnaghi's in Bond Street on the opening day of an exhibition and people scrambled in to buy. The Royal Academy, however, ignored him: so did the critics. He painted both in oils and watercolour, both portraits and landscapes. He could catch a quick likeness with a touch of de Laszlo's panache, but landscape was his primary interest. He was extremely sympathetic to the wind-driven skies and the shimmering marshes of Norfolk. His brush was very facile, his colours pure and mysteriously life-enhancing. He was light years away from all that was fashionable with the world of art or of Blooms-

A photograph by Prince Philip of Edward Seago at work in the Antarctic during 'Britannia's' 1956–57 cruise

bury. He was, however, securely locked in the tradition of the great East Anglian painters, a true descendant of old Crome and Constable who are now revered. In the forties he painted a lively portrait of King George VI, and did three impressionistic studies of the wedding procession of Princess Elizabeth and Lieutenant Mountbatten. By then he was in high favour with all members of the Royal Family, and Queen Elizabeth, the Queen Mother, invited him to Sandringham in January 1950. For the next twenty-two years he visited Sandringham regularly both in winter and summer and the Royal Family acquired numerous dazzling Seagos. And then in 1956 Prince Philip invited Seago to accompany him to the Antarctic on board the *Britannia*. Seago accepted. During the voyage he gave lessons to the Prince in watercolour painting and produced a series of fascinating Antarctic landscapes that are now part of the royal collections. Some are at Balmoral, some, rightly, at Sandringham, but Seago remains the only artist of quality to have painted these strange lunar landscapes of the far South. Later he gave lessons to the Prince of Wales. Both father and son greatly admired his skill and creative energy and they loved his pictures. This royal support was extremely important to Seago who was a deeply insecure man, wounded by the neglect and hostility not only of art critics but also of the artistic establishment as represented by the Royal Academy. As well as strengthening his confidence, the royal patronage also gave him opportunities to paint landscapes of countries he would never have seen or visited. One can argue that Seago was not in the class of a Sutherland, or Bacon, or Hitchens and

*Edward Seago: Antarctic Scene
and '"The John Biscoe" in
the Antarctic'*

'Evening on the Hard, Pin
Mill' and 'West African
Market, Selikini'

many other painters of deeper creative talent, but he was thoroughly accomplished in a deeply English tradition and his work will be remembered long after the brick arrangers, the minimalists and the rest are forgotten. His talents were fostered by Queen Mary, by Queen Elizabeth, the Queen Mother, and by Prince Philip, and it was patronage well placed.

The same policy has been adopted to works of art as with paintings. Desirable additions to the collection are found by detailed examination of catalogues and exhibitions. The principal additions of works of art are objects associated with previous monarchs and a very remarkable feature of this policy is how, even today, objects may turn up that belonged to monarchs who lived centuries ago. Recently the hunting knives of Henry VIII were discovered and secured for the collection. These rare and distinguished objects are now displayed on the Grand Staircase at Windsor.

Equally rare and perhaps more immediately impressive are the two caddinets which belonged to King William III and Queen Mary II. Caddinets were not uncommon in Europe, where they were used on state occasions not only by royalty but also by the higher peerage and other distinguished members of the Court, but they tended to be used only when dining with people of almost equal rank – at least in France, according to St Simon, the chronicler, for whom all the finer points of etiquette were honey to the soul.

Caddinets were, it seems, exceptionally rare in England. There is no mention of their being used by any monarch before Charles II who had one placed before him at his Coronation Banquet. In Hanoverian times their use was forgotten. In 1782 there were three in the royal plate collection (maybe these two and another). By 1832, when a full inventory of the royal plate was taken, they had all vanished. The two that now survive belonged to the Earl of Lonsdale and he probably bought them when George IV sold off a lot of old royal plate in 1808. Now they have returned to the fold and are on view with the Crown Jewels at the Tower.

They are silver-gilt – one made in 1683–4, the other in 1688–9 by Anthony Nelme, the Huguenot silversmith. They are both beautifully engraved with the royal arms and almost certainly they were prepared for the Coronation of William and Mary in 1689 and they stood before them at the Coronation Banquet, to give added state to the King and Queen. At the side of them is a compartment or box for the royal cutlery as well as space for a small compartment for salt. The workmanship and engraving are in the great tradition of Huguenot silversmiths, and these very rare objects make a worthy addition to the Jewel House.

Dame Barbara Hepworth: 'Arthrodesis of the hip'

Ivon Hitchens: 'Firwood Ride – Gentle Spring' (Windsor Castle)

Paul Nash: 'Tamaris Well' (Sandringham)

Edward Seago: 'Buckingham Palace from St James's
Park' (Watercolour, Windsor Castle)
Sir Winston Churchill: 'Palladian Bridge' (Windsor
Castle)
The collection is particularly rich in modern landscape
paintings

Some acquisitions throw light on the development of the palaces and are of first importance in research about royal buildings. This was the reason for the purchase of drawings by Morel and Seddon making suggestions for the interior arrangements of George IV's private apartments at Windsor in the 1820s when he was renovating the Castle. Likewise the design of a curtain rod by Pugin. The policy with regard to works of art is, therefore, to strengthen the collection where there are gaps or to buy objects which lead to greater understanding of the past. But, as with paintings, there remains the question of the patronage of modern craftsmen – glass engravers such as Laurence Whistler, or fine silversmiths such as Gerald Benney from whom the Queen commissioned several pieces. Such patronage is important to the collection as well as to the craftsmen, otherwise this reign would have little to contribute to the future. Even at the present time an exhibition could easily be mounted to display the high quality of modern British craftsmanship in all the major fields – furniture, silver, porcelain, glass and textiles. A splendid example of the latter is the new carpet for the Garter Throne Room at Windsor Castle which has been selected by the Queen from designs submitted by the students at Bradford Technical College.

In periods of great art, in periods of abysmal art, one type of patronage must always be undertaken – the state portrait. It is traditional that the monarch should be painted in his or her Robes of State as soon as possible after the Coronation. Indeed, the privy councillors of Elizabeth I were so worried about the possibility of unofficial representation of the Queen being made that they issued a proclamation forbidding all pictures of the Queen until the official portrait was available. Queen Elizabeth I was very fortunate in having the great painter, Nicholas Hilliard; George III in Allan Ramsay. Queen Elizabeth II was less fortunate, but in Sir James Gunn she had at least a highly skilled portrait painter, if no genius. One state portrait leads to other portraits: every society of which the Queen is patron, every regiment of which she is colonel, and all the embassies want an official portrait. No year goes by without an official portrait of some kind or another being painted. Some are best left unmentioned, others prove disappointing – as with the Annigoni painted for the National Portrait Gallery, a portrait which manages to kill all the warmth and happiness of the Queen's temperament. (He was, perhaps, more successful with Prince Philip who obviously admires his own portrait for it hangs in his study at Windsor.) However, many succeed, and perhaps one of the best is by Michael Noakes, who also drew a brilliant preliminary sketch for this picture which the Prince of Wales bought. It now hangs in his sitting-room at Windsor Castle. However,

Alan Davie: 'Throne of the Eye Goddess'. One of the modern British paintings acquired for the rooms for guests in the Edward III Tower, Windsor Castle

the majority of the portraits of the Queen or of Prince Philip have not been for the Royal Collection. Indeed there are fewer portraits of them than of previous monarchs and consorts. That is a pity.

Not only is the Queen painted time and time again for official portraits but, in accordance with tradition, the important rituals in which she takes part are also painted. The Coronation procession was painted by Topolski, and so was the Coronation itself by Terence Cuneo – just as Queen Victoria's was painted by Leslie and Hayter, or Edward VII's by

Pietro Annigoni: Studies for portraits of the Queen (facing) and Princess Margaret

Abbey, but she was not served as well as either of them. She has been painted 'Trooping the Colour' as well as 'Opening Parliament'. The Jubilee procession was painted and the great events of her reign will be immortalised in this traditional way, extending the collection along lines laid down by history itself. Poor art they may often be, but most valuable for the historical record.

There is, however, one gap in this tradition. There are brilliant royal group paintings in the collections – very fine ones by Winterhalter of Queen Victoria, Prince Albert and their children; delightful Zoffanys of George III, Queen Charlotte and their family; haunting van Dycks of Charles I's wife and children. Even the last reign witnessed one or two splendid conversation pieces – the Gunn of King George VI, Queen Elizabeth and the Princesses at tea in the drawing-room at Royal Lodge, and a brilliant Seago where Princess Margaret is playing the piano. Unfortunately there are no similar conversation pieces of this reign. There are photographs of the Royal Family by Lord Snowdon but, excellent as they are, they do not fill the gap. Painters of good conversation pieces are rarer even than good portrait painters but they are not extinct: perhaps they may yet be used.

Lord Snowdon: Photographs of two generations.
Opposite: The Queen with Prince Charles and Princess Anne
Left: Princess Anne with Captain Mark Phillips and Master Peter Phillips

Denis Fildes: Queen Elizabeth
(The Queen Mother)

Reid Dick: King George VI,
1954

Edwin Brock: The young Princess Elizabeth

Anita Lafford: Prince Charles

Above: Sir William Dobell:
'Country Race Meeting'.
Right: The Duke of Edinburgh
during filming on the stairs of the
Edward III Tower, Windsor Castle,
with Sir Russell Drysdale's 'Man in
a Landscape' and the Dobell below.
The collection is particularly rich in
works by Australian artists

Above: Sidney Nolan: 'Herd at the Waterhole'. There are several paintings by Nolan in the collection, including 'Strange Fruit' and a landscape in the drawing-room of the Edward III Tower

During a 1956 visit to Australia, Prince Philip went to Alice Springs where he bought a number of landscapes of central Australia by aboriginal artists. Among them are two watercolours by Albert Namatjira, one of the leading artists of this school ('Australian Landscape' bottom left). In 1963 Prince Philip acquired two watercolours by Rex Batterbee, who had originally encouraged and advised the aboriginal artists and whose influence can be clearly seen in their work ('Centralian Ghost Gum' top left)

CHAPTER FOUR

RESTORATION AND RENEWAL

Certain royal residences such as Hampton Court or the Tower of London are no longer lived in by the Royal Family and so can be treated as if they were museums – humidity and heat can be controlled, lighting properly subdued or directed to particular objects or pictures. But the great majority of royal residences are lived in and worked in: people sit in chairs; the light is what is necessary for living, not what is best for pictures; windows are opened; china and silver are used, so is glass; clocks must function; carpets are trodden on. Even historic carriages have to be able to work: indeed they are constantly in use fetching ambassadors to present their credentials, conveying members of the Royal Family to Victoria Station to meet Heads of State or to the Opening of Parliament, or on royal occasions outside London. In the summer of 1979, for example, the Queen Mother drove in the Irish State coach through Dover on her inauguration as Warden of the Cinque Ports.

Leonard Knyff: 'Birdseye View of Hampton Court' (Detail). This interesting painting was acquired during the reign of King George VI, and is an invaluable record of the Palace at the beginning of the eighteenth century. From left to right it shows the wrought-iron screen of Tijou, the new parterres and avenues in the French style, and Sir Christopher Wren's east façade

The wear and tear might be a little less severe on the royal possessions if visitors were merely heads of state or came in small numbers, but many royal occasions are vast. Over 20,000 visitors a year tramp over the carpets in the Bow Room during the summer months as they go through Buckingham Palace to the garden parties. The Diplomatic Evening Reception at the Palace sees the state rooms, including the Picture Gallery, crowded with guests. At a state banquet at which the incomparable Sèvres services are used, there are over a hundred guests to seat and serve. Hence most of the objects in the royal collections are subject to wear and tear that the directors of a great museum would never tolerate but which must be accepted in the royal palaces. This adds an extra dimension of concern to those who keep the collections in a fine state of repair.

And the monarchs, too, and their consorts have, sometimes, very strong views of what is to be done with furnishings or buildings. In previous generations the idea of conservation was far less strong. Edward VII disliked many of the carefully planned arrangements and furnishings of Queen Victoria and Prince Albert at Buckingham Palace and Windsor and changed them drastically – and rarely, if ever, to advantage. Again, Queen Mary, who had many admirable qualities, including a deep love of antiques, had not much of an eye for the placing of an Old Master and under her command the Picture Gallery at Buckingham Palace became a terrible jumble. The war in this respect was a boon for these great pictures were taken down for safety's sake and despatched to Wales, to be stored there with pictures from the National Gallery. After the war this created an opportunity for the gallery to be redecorated in colours far kinder to pictures, and for them to be rehung to show many masterpieces to a far better advantage. What may seem sensible to one age can appear idiotic to another.

Of course, previous generations did not regard their contemporary artists with the reverence that we now accord them. If pictures did not fit, they might be adjusted: this was commonplace in the eighteenth century in order to balance the size of the pictures – at least two royal Rubenses suffered in this way. A badly damaged painting might be almost totally repainted. George III bought a staggering number of Canalettos – fifty-three in all – from Consul Smith in 1762 to decorate the walls of Buckingham House which he had just bought for his wife. The blue of the sky was regarded as too Mediterranean possibly either by George III or by his advisers so it was toned down to a darker colour on all the pictures. Now the toning down is having to be painstakingly removed centimetre by centimetre and the glorious Venetian blues of Canaletto are once more seeing the light of day.

The task facing the Surveyors and the Librarian is a formidable one. The sheer size of the collection is so daunting – over 5000 oil paintings have to be cared for; there are nearly 30,000 Old Master drawings and watercolours; there are tens of thousands of books and manuscripts, some of exceptional rarity and very considerable age. There is the greatest collection of Sèvres china in the world and one of the greatest collections of old English china, too. Armour, stamps, furniture are equally abundant. The plate rooms are, and had to be, very large. Indeed it is almost impossible to give a correct idea of the extent of the task which faces the superintendents of the palaces and the Surveyors who are in charge of the various parts of the collection.

There is a further difficulty which now preoccupies those responsible. Many objects are moving into what might be called critical old age. Throughout the nineteenth century Buckingham Palace was comparatively new; Kensington Palace older but not very old; Balmoral, Osborne and Sandringham, indeed, brand new. They have now had over a hundred years of constant use. The same is true of furnishings – the French furniture purchased by George IV was in the same dimension of time to Queen Victoria as Art Deco might be to the Queen today. Hence it was treated with less reverence, used more extensively and, in consequence, suffered. Further problems have been caused by the changes in the technology of living: central heating dries the atmosphere and causes wood to warp: unless the wood can move naturally the result is likely to be a split, a crack or a violent distortion. Not only furniture suffers badly but so do paintings, for many Old Masters were painted on wooden panels. To put in sophisticated humidifying equipment throughout the royal palaces would be an impossible expense, and in any case much of the damage had been done before humidity control was properly understood. There are many other technical problems of this kind. The leather packing essential to make armour bearable to wear dries out over the centuries, becomes friable and finally disappears unless carefully preserved. Glue used on mounts of Old Master drawings can grow discoloured with age and do great harm to the drawings themselves, which is why the Victorian backings of the great Leonardo drawings are being torn off – a method which requires skill and nerve. Wherever one looks there are problems of renewal and restoration.

There is one further development which has had an important influence on the care of the royal buildings. Probably royal servants always lived in better conditions than those in private service, but by modern standards these conditions would no longer be acceptable. Also royal administration has grown over the last half century like every other administration with a far greater proportion of secretaries and secretarial assistants than ever before. Everyone expects better conditions, rightly so, and naturally the monarchs of this century have wished to be, as Queen Victoria and Prince Albert were, amongst the foremost in providing first-class amenities for their staff – not only during their employment but also for their old age. Prince Albert built a number of pensioners' houses at Osborne, for their time exceptionally commodious and well appointed, and he did the same at Balmoral. Every Queen from Queen Alexandra to Queen Elizabeth II has built cottages at Sandringham for retired staff and in addition the Queen has added further blocks of pensioners' houses at Balmoral. The staff, during their working lives, expect and deserve improved conditions, and space had to be made in Windsor and at Buckingham Palace for recreation centres, dining-rooms and rest areas, and this had to be done without encroachment on the historic nature of the buildings. This posed very difficult problems for the architect. What has been done – particularly in Buckingham Palace – has been exceptionally well done. The staff dining-rooms are commodious, very efficient and attractively decorated by a display of china. The entrance to the senior staff dining-room has a fascinatingly mixed display of bisque china, some Victorian pottery, copper utensils and very nostalgic porcelain menu tablets dating from the reign of Edward VII. Also working conditions for all staff had to be improved in several palaces, but notably at Sandringham. The endless warren of small rooms and the antiquated kitchens there had to be replaced and modernised, and so the opportunity was taken to modify not only the working quarters but also some of Sandringham House itself. The result is up-to-date, highly efficient kitchens and a much smaller house. This type of modification which improves efficiency and cuts heating and maintenance costs is a constant preoccupation of the Royal Family and their Household. Royal residences, therefore, are not fixed like flies in amber but are living, changing institutions; their historic qualities are carefully preserved but these palaces and houses have to conform to the standards of their time and also meet the challenges posed by a world of inflation and shortages of trained staff.

Similar challenges have been posed by the estates themselves. The land surrounding Windsor, Balmoral and Sandringham has to fulfil a dual purpose: it must provide an appropriate aesthetic setting for the royal residence, and it must be as productive as possible in a way that does not jar on aesthetic sensitivities. Efficient estate management has been for centuries a part of the royal tradition.

James I employed Vermuyden, the famous Dutch engineer, to drain the swampy forest land that formed so much of the Windsor Great Park at that time. He also planted an avenue of mulberry trees which still exists. He hoped to start the silk industry in England – the silkworms live on mulberry leaves – but, alas, the King obtained and planted the wrong type of mulberry. George III, however, was the King who really tackled the improvement of agriculture at Windsor. With the help of Nathaniel Kent, he created two farms in the Great Park, both with very revealing names – the Flemish Farm and the Norfolk Farm: Flanders and Norfolk were thought to have the most advanced and efficient farming techniques of the time: indeed modern scientific farming stems from their experiments. George III became passionately interested in these farms and thought nothing of taking a thirteen-mile walk to inspect them. Prince Albert, who was made Deputy Ranger of the Park by Queen Victoria, brought the same high intelligence and efficiency to farming as he did to everything else. He planned and rebuilt the old farms and provided for better housing for the workers. He was indefatigable in promoting agricultural machinery – including a steam plough – and he was very concerned to improve the stock: his dairy farm was, in his words, 'the best cow house in the world' and it is still very much in use today. His son and grandson were less interested.

The troubled decade of the thirties, followed by the war, left many problems at Sandringham, Balmoral and, above all, Windsor. The Great Park had gone under the plough. Fuel shortages had led to the closure of greenhouses, and closed greenhouses steadily decay. Time, as always, had taken its toll. Techniques which were efficient and up-to-date in the 1920s were hopelessly archaic in the 1950s. The style of life in the royal palaces had also changed: there were fewer staff; consumption had become more economic and less lavish; even the fashion in food had changed. Edward VII had liked quail for his breakfast or even cold partridge: indeed the Edwardians and Georgians had loved a super-abundance of exotic fruit and out-of-season vegetables which were difficult and expensive to produce. However, what had been rare and difficult in the twenties, had, because of air transport, become commonplace and cheap by the fifties. There was a great need to develop a policy of renewal for the glasshouses as well as the estates surrounding the royal residences. This has been one of the preoccupations of Prince Philip.

At Sandringham the Home Farm has been completely reorganised and made productive and profitable. One of the great crops produced is blackcurrants which go to the Ribena makers; another is a delicious variety of Cox's Orange Pippin apple for which people drive hundreds of

miles. Forestry and land reclamation have been two other important developments. The virtue of the efficient exploitation of the 3400-acre Home Farm has been that profits were available for the renewal of buildings, and the grounds of Sandringham could be renewed and restored to the great benefit not only of the Royal Family but also the public. As we shall see there was money to develop museums and new areas for the enjoyment of visitors.

The same efficiency was brought to bear on Windsor. The first important step was to turn the Park back from arable to grass. Prince Philip reintroduced deer, which had been removed by the needs of war. After all, deer had roamed in the Great Park since the Conquest; the new herd was brought from Balmoral. The Park itself, with its distant and splendid vistas of the Castle, was a favourite picnic ground for many visitors and, with their ever-increasing numbers, new picnic areas and amenities were essential. But there were other problems at Windsor – Queen Victoria's enormous glasshouses were at the end of their tether; the view from the East Terrace was not satisfactory; there was no small private garden adjacent to the royal apartments; no provision had been

Paul Sandby: 'Windsor Castle from the North-east, the River Thames in the foreground'

made for the wildlife of the Park which, in an increasingly dangerous chemical world, were at risk. The Prince Consort, an estate manager himself of great efficiency, would have been delighted by the rapid progress that was made in the fifties, a progress which has continued during the sixties and seventies until now the Windsor Park and Home Farms are a model of efficiency.

The vista from the East Terrace has been greatly improved: it now stretches away into the Park, green blending with green and in the distance the darker trees, but utility is combined with beauty. The glasshouses posed a difficult problem. They could have been reduced in size, but instead it was decided to build new ones. With their automatic ventilation, light controls, feeding and irrigation systems, they are some of the most modern in Europe, requiring only a fraction of the staff that the miles of old wooden glasshouses required. They provide not only all the flowers for Windsor Castle and Buckingham Palace but also a surplus for sale to the public. Similarly there is a highly productive and profitable mushroom farm. This efficiency, of course, is reflected in the condition of the immediate surroundings of the Castle and of the Castle itself. Never before have they attained such a high standard of repair. Both Windsor and Sandringham are model country estates run in the most up-to-date and efficient way.

Restoration and renewal, of course, is a never-ending process – once the ravages of war were overcome then attention could be given to less urgent needs and an attempt made to break the huge backlog of repairs and improvements. A new wall display of armour was created in the Guard Chamber, Vestibule and Grand Entrance at Windsor, the geo-metric patterns on the wall were inspired by the seventeenth-century arrangements of armour at Hampton Court and elsewhere at Windsor. More recently the splendid Willis organ, which is used not only on the formal occasions but sometimes for duets by Prince Edward and Lady Sarah Armstrong-Jones, was completely dismantled. Its pipes were so multitudinous that they covered much of the St George's Hall, but the cleaning and restoration were long overdue and the improvement was spectacular. At the present time another improvement is taking place under the supervision of Prince Philip. The Holbein Room was a dark, rather sepulchral place; it is now being opened up and repainted and will make a much better gallery for the early royal portraits when they are rehung. Prince Albert hung them all there more like icons than pictures. The less important portraits have been weeded out and the finer ones are now displayed as they should be. The octagonal Private Chapel, next door, has been redecorated and refurnished by Sir Hugh Casson, and this

Working on the Roentgen desk in the Marlborough House workshops

will improve the flow from the State Apartments to St George's Hall.

Such work never ends. There are always rooms in need of decoration, of improvement, of restoration, and this is true of Buckingham Palace as it is of Windsor, and sometimes, of course, these improvements and restorations are a major undertaking. One of the most interesting of the small rooms at Buckingham Palace is the Chinese Dining Room. Queen Victoria and Prince Albert found the Brighton Pavilion impossible to live in because the crowds 'mobbed' them and they could obtain no privacy. And so they abandoned Brighton in 1847. At this time they were building the front that we know at Buckingham Palace. They decided to create a Chinese Dining Room in the corner which overlooks the Mall and the room was constructed to take a variety of fine decorations from rooms in the Pavilion. Since then it has been in constant use: Queen Victoria liked it as a luncheon room; other monarchs have used it occasionally for the same purpose but more frequently for meetings. Years passed, decades passed, a century passed and the second one began to tick away: the carpet, designed by Ludwig Grüner, the Prince Consort's artistic adviser, began to wear out; the wall decorations grew darker and darker; the lustre of the gold leaf dimmed; the silk in the pelmets rotted; the dragons, alas, began to chip – bits dropped off their beaks or claws or serrated wings. The whole room had got to the point where thorough restoration was essential. One of the greatest chinoiserie rooms in England could not last for ever without repairs and renovation.

Paul Sandby: 'South-east view of Windsor Castle from the Home Park', a recent acquisition. This eighteenth-century artist who spent much of his time at Windsor is particularly well represented. The collection of drawings in the Print Room of the Royal Library numbers over 23,000, and includes important holdings of major artists such as Leonardo da Vinci, Holbein and Canaletto

Graham Sutherland: 'Fight between Workers and Drones'

Peter Blake: 'Study of Puck'

8.15 p.m.

8.45 p.m.

9.15 p.m.

11.15 p.m.

1 a.m.

3 a.m.

June 10th 1971 — for His Royal Highness Prince Philip, Duke of Edinburgh —

So the entire room has been dismantled: the great brilliantly coloured vases which stood between the windows have been lifted from their pedestals; the pelmets with their rioting golden dragons have been carefully taken down; the wooden painted dragons have been removed from the legs of the side tables. The workshops that are located in the basement of Buckingham Palace are being taxed to the limit of their skill. The embroiderers have to repair the heavy yellow and silver braid that has disintegrated with age. Almost all the silk has gone for good, so the appliqué dragons, carefully restored, are stitched back on to a base the same colour as the silk but less expensive and more durable. This is exacting work and requires considerable skill from the craftswomen who do the embroidery but they will be proud of their work when the pelmets and hangings are back in place. And so, too, will be the craftsmen. They are having to make the most delicate beaks and tiny bits of wings to replace those which have crumbled into dust over the years. Some of the fretwork panels too have gone: these were in boxwood, plentiful in the Prince Regent's day, very scarce and not at all cheap today, but any other wood would jar by its difference – unlike the substitution for the silk – so boxwood has had to be found. Whilst the craftsmen are carving, gilding and repairing, the picture restorers from the Department of the Environment, which is responsible for the fabric of royal buildings, are at work in the room itself, cleaning the splendid dragon that riots across the ceiling on its billowing clouds, bringing to light again the brilliant blues of the sky and the deep blood red of so much of the decorations. The wall pictures, cleaned of the varnish of a century, stand out boldly in all the radiance of their colouring.

The old carpet, too costly to repeat, is being replaced. The Queen will choose the colour and design and it will be specially woven. When fully restored the room will have recovered its splendid bravura and fantasy – a relic of Brighton Pavilion, the most original of all royal residences, tucked away behind the monumental and somewhat pompous façade of Buckingham Palace – a delectable surprise for all who have the privilege of stepping inside it. If only the tiny golden bells that decorate so much of the room, as bright now as when they were made, would tinkle a welcome!

Time, combined with central heating over the last half-century, can create far greater problems than those found in the Chinese Dining Room, demanding in their solution even greater skills. The furniture which has suffered most from central heating is the late seventeenth- and eighteenth-century French furniture which both Windsor Castle and Buckingham Palace have in abundance, thanks to George IV's gar-

Sir Hugh Casson is renowned for his illustrated letters, and in this one sends his thanks to the Duke of Edinburgh for an enjoyable evening party at Buckingham Palace

gantuan appetite for it. Most of this furniture has now reached an age where problems multiply – once central heating has caused a warp or a crack, others will soon follow.

The eighteenth century loved mechanical contrivances in furniture, particularly desks, and the Royal Collection has a superb specimen, made by the great *ébéniste*, Roentgen. It is oak, veneered in mahogany, and the lid is cylindrical in shape: a system of locks which trigger springs puts the mechanism in action and this works very largely through delicately poised counterweights. Once the springs are triggered, the curved lid rolls back, doors fly open, slides come forward: all should work as smoothly as silk. Roentgen realised the dangers of heat and cold and much of the basic frame is made of intricate blocks of oak that allow for a certain amount of expansion and contraction. What they never counted on was the effect of central heating or the effect of accumulated dust of a century or more on the complex internal metal mechanisms. Although much of the base of the desk allowed for contraction and expansion the oak lining of the lid did not, so a great crack now runs across the cylindrical lid, warping the veneer and, of course, preventing the mechanism from operating. In other places, too, the veneer has taken the toll of time. So the whole desk has had to be carefully dismantled, the mechanism cleaned, the veneers replaced when too damaged, and careful adjustments made to the cylinder lining so that it will give and adjust to heat without cracking: all of this work required the greatest skill and was undertaken by craftsmen at the workshops in Marlborough House.

They struggle against great difficulties for the rare woods in which the French craftsmen took such delight are becoming very scarce – harewood, boxwood, lemon wood, laburnum, rosewood and many others are almost unobtainable. When available the veneers are now cut so thinly by the timber merchants that the craftsmen run into other difficulties. Fortunately, about the royal palaces, in lumber rooms and attics, a certain amount of broken furniture has accumulated – commodes, chairs, desks, battered beyond any hope of repair, the shipwrecks of time. So they are cannibalised, as it were – bits and pieces of them being incorporated in the restored desk or commode or chair.

For craftsmen of such skill the restoration of the Roentgen desk is a moderately easy task, even though immensely time-consuming; but earlier furniture, particularly Boulle of the seventeenth century, presents greater problems, as do some of the lacquered and *pietra dura* furnishings. The Italian cabinet-makers, many of whom emigrated to France in the late sixteenth and seventeenth centuries, were masters of the *pietra dura* techniques. But time is no kinder to this type of furniture than to the highly veneered carpentry of the eighteenth century. The craftsmen use varied coloured marbles and other hard stones to decorate table tops with designs of flowers or scrolls or arabesques; sometimes the front of a cabinet is similarly decorated. Naturally the stone has to be very finely cut or the weight would be intolerable; the slate base to which the stones are fixed must be thin too, unless it is for a stout table. Thinness means fragility: stones crack or become dislodged; fractures in the base plate cause distortion; sometimes the flowers and scrolls become very distorted; and age discolours the stone. Another formidable restoration problem occurs. As in many other situations, the work of earlier restorers can make matters worse — hasty replacements, patching that is badly done. The only safe method is to strip the piece of furniture: to take off all the pieces of marble one by one. This has to be done with extreme care as the marble is thin and easily broken. Fortunately the Italian craftsmen always drew their designs on the base plates of slate, at times indicating the colour of the marble to be used. When reassembled, with the marbles cleaned, the furniture appears in all its richness and grandeur, sparkling with colour.

As with *pietra dura* so with *boulle*, which is full of technical difficulties for the restorer. The major decoration element in *boulle* is tortoise-shell: two types of shell are used — the back of the shell with its variegated browns and yellows, and the belly shell which is translucent. The translucent shell allows decorative colour to appear through it, hence giving greater variety to the *boulle* technique. The shell is usually set in brass, but also in pewter, which does not age gracefully: it develops white scales that powder, the belly shell discolours and becomes opaque, and the colour beneath is lost. Occasionally the pewter crumbles so far that bits of shell fall out, and these can get misplaced or vanish altogether. As with *pietra dura*, restoration is very highly skilled and difficult; difficult, too, because shell is in exceedingly short supply, particularly the belly shell where the main requirement falls. But when the restoration is complete, the result is startling and beautiful. The *boulle* cabinet-makers very frequently used a brilliant lapis lazuli blue under the belly shell which, when it re-emerges into the light of day, changes the whole aspect of the furniture. Unrestored *boulle* looks dead and leaden, forbidding almost, and conjures up a court heavy with the rectitude of Madame de Maintenon and Louis XIV in their old age, whereas restored *boulle* has the glitter and sparkle, the air of Louis XIV's youth. One of the outstanding pieces of furniture in the Royal Collection is a cabinet veneered with marquetry in *boulle*. This has now been restored to its pristine beauty and glows again with the blue of lapis lazuli.

All of this highly skilled work is in the hands of three craftsmen who work in a smallish room at Marlborough House. Nearby is another craftsman who sometimes aids them with their metal work but whose principal job is to restore the armour – including, of course, the firearms, as well as the swords and suits of armour. The problem with armour lies in the leather rather than the metal. Leather is essential for the joints and of course for lining, but leather crumbles. Modern buff leather (the type of leather always used) is far thicker than that used by the Tudors and Stuarts which causes extra problems. The great and terrifying suit of armour of Henry VIII brooded over the recent Holbein exhibition like a symbol of destiny. But it only stood in so threatening a posture – upright and together – because the leather had all been replaced just before the exhibition took place. After leather, the major problem is often the thin silver wire used to bind the grip of swords: it becomes friable with age. Another frequent problem is found in the butts of hand guns which were usually made of walnut and liable to be infested with woodworm which find walnut a delectable dish. As there are thousands of swords, guns, pikes, claymores, sabres and pieces of armour in the collection, the one restorer has work for eternity.

Most of this restoration work comes under the aegis of the Surveyor of the Queen's Works of Art, Mr Geoffrey de Bellaigue, and he occasionally obtains a small bonus from the work apart from the delight of seeing a fine decaying piece of furniture given a new lease of life. Restorers can confirm scholarly hunches, for cabinet-makers often signed their works in the most inaccessible places. When a *pietra dura* commode was dismantled some time ago, underneath the marbles was the Italian maker's signature – Giachetti – a maker who Sir Francis Watson, one of the leading authorities on antique furniture, thought was responsible, but now the attribution is absolute.

Scholarship of the most exacting kind often lies at the heart of this type of restoration work: scholarship about the craft itself – the intentions of the cabinet-makers or armourers must be precisely known, also the way they deployed their skills and the tools which they used; and knowledge of materials must be as exact as theirs. Equally important is the positioning of much of the furniture. In the past rooms were decorated and adorned with particular types of furniture in mind, hence the need to search old records not merely for authenticity and provenance, important as they are, but to discover also the setting for which the piece was designed so that it can be placed in its proper historical context.

An even greater dependence on scholarship of every kind is necessary in the restoration of pictures or the treatment of drawings. Although there was considerable copying of fine French furniture in the early nineteenth century, the question of authenticity is not so acute as with pictures. As has been mentioned, carpenters signed their work in obscure and inaccessible places which restoration reveals; this could obviously not be true of pictures, and Old Master drawings are only rarely signed. Naturally provenance – knowing where the cabinet or picture came from and when – is important for both classes of object and this requires long searches in the archives for bills, inventories and other documentary material, and not only in British archives. The French archives are a very rich source for all the French decorative arts – furniture, sculpture, bronzes, carpets and, above all, for Sèvres china.

Sèvres china was very skilfully faked throughout the nineteenth century, and the question of authenticity of a particular piece requires considerable research. Mr Geoffrey de Bellaigue's work on Sèvres china in the Royal Collection is particularly outstanding. The archives at the factory itself are very rich: the sales ledgers extend from 1752, and also from the earliest period of its manufacture the chief Parisian dealer, Lazare Duvaux, kept a very detailed journal of what he sold and to whom. These sources, although they can rarely, if ever, tie down a piece of the Queen's Sèvres to a precise sale on a given date, can demonstrate that vases of such a shape with similar decoration and in the identical colour were being produced at the date marked on the china itself, for most Sèvres is precisely dated. Also most of this china has a painter's mark, and whether such a painter was painting such china with the subjects with which it is decorated can be verified from the factory's own archives. This raises probability high but it can be taken a stage further to certainty. It could be argued that every process, here described, could be faked if the faker copied a genuine piece exactly and that is true. However, there is a further test, which was invented by the Danish scholar Svend Eriksen. The potters and painters incised marks on the china they were making before it was fired. These signs look meaningless but if they are catalogued from pieces we know to be genuine, and it can be shown that they recur many times in genuine pieces, then it is most improbable that any faker would get them right. In fact, fakers practically never used incised marks at all. Genuine pieces are, for example, the magnificent service that was ordered for Louis XVI and then sold to George IV when he was Prince of Wales. We know the detailed history of this service from the time it was clay until it adorned George IV's table, apart from a brief period between 1794 and 1811. And there are many

other services that were French royal gifts that have remained in the hands of descendants ever since, whose marks can be used in a similar way. Such detective work helps to authenticate pieces about which the royal archives themselves are silent, and, on occasion, leads to the identification of the men or women who painted them.

But the full range of technical skills and scholarship really come into play with paintings. The faking of art is almost as old as art itself. The Romans faked Greek sculpture; in the Renaissance Italian sculptors faked Roman fakes of Greek; by 1750 there were more faked Rembrandts than genuine ones; almost as soon as Raphael was dead, skilful fakes were being painted by contemporaries; and so it has gone on down to our own day. The fakes, of course, have got steadily better – no faker now would start on a Rembrandt panel without making sure that the wood was contemporary with Rembrandt himself, but to do that would present him with great difficulties and he would have to take a bit of a chance or destroy a picture of value because the science of dendrochronology (dating of wood) has become extremely precise. The science of pigmentation is also very exact for the chemical constitution of paint has changed a great deal over the centuries. X-ray cameras can now disclose what is beneath the surface of a picture. All of these new scientific methods may come into play when a painting is being investigated, but the work of scholarship has to begin with books and records. There is not much point in subjecting a picture to elaborate and expensive investigation if the records themselves cast doubt on its authenticity.

With over 5000 oil paintings in the Royal Collection there is considerable scope for scholarship. In previous centuries inventories of them were made; some were very good, others were more haphazard, and even the descriptions or titles, at times, were so cursory that they could not be applied to any picture. The Prince Consort saw the necessity for a more systematic approach and initiated the great inventory of pictures which was compiled by Richard Redgrave. Several catalogues of the more important pictures were produced. These were, however, very selective and concerned with the contents of particular palaces. More systematic and scholarly catalogues of both paintings and drawings, categorised by schools of painters rather than palaces, began only in the 1930s with the major work on the Old Master drawings. Eighteen volumes have been published so far – the work of scholars of international renown. Rudolph Wittkower, one of the leading art historians of his time, published *The Drawings of the Carracci*; Sir John Pope-Hennessy, who was Director of the Victoria and Albert Museum and subsequently of the British Museum, was responsible for the very large catalogue, with 1758 entries, of

Sèvres pot pourri vase and cover, 1758

Domenichino's drawings. One of the great glories of the Old Master drawing collection is the great series of Leonardos, which were catalogued by Lord Clark in collaboration with the Italian scholar, Carlo Pedretti. A further stage in publication has now been undertaken with the Leonardos, which are being reproduced magnificently in facsimile – a development which one hopes will be followed by volumes dedicated to other Masters. The work of cataloguing, however, is still far from complete and the work steadily progresses.

Fewer volumes of catalogues of paintings have so far been produced. They are based on careful examination of the pictures themselves, combined with research work in the Royal Archives and in the Public Record Office and British Library where there are bills, inventories, early lists and descriptions by those who saw them long ago. The results are outstanding works of scholarship. Sir Oliver Millar, the Surveyor of the Queen's Pictures, has produced two parts of the new catalogue, one dealing with *Tudor, Stuart and Early Georgian Pictures in the Royal Collection* (1963), and the other with *Later Georgian Pictures* (1969). Now he is at work on a sequel which will cover the nineteenth-century pictures. His wife is working on the Victorian collection of drawings and watercolours. As with the Old Master drawings, distinguished scholars have undertaken some of this work. *Later Italian Pictures* was commissioned from Michael Levey, the present Director of the National Gallery. Christopher White of Yale has almost completed a catalogue of the Dutch pictures, a very large number of which came into royal possession through George IV, and the provenance and previous history of the pictures often requires the most painstaking detective work in Dutch archives. In paintings and in drawings, the scholarship that has been applied to the Royal Collection is comparable to any in the world. Another important volume which is almost complete is John Shearman's *Early Italian Pictures.*

In addition to the catalogues, other research work of great importance is undertaken: some of this was incorporated in Sir Oliver Millar's one-volume survey of the collection, *The Queen's Pictures*, published in 1977 for the Queen's Jubilee; other results are to be found in the scholarly volumes on Charles I's collection published by the Walpole Society. Much of this work is made possible by the fact that the Surveyorship is no longer a part-time employment.

Alas, the decorative arts have not yet been so well served. Just before World War I, Laking produced a number of important catalogues on the furniture, the armour and the Sèvres porcelain, and E. H. Jones on the

The temporary restoration studio in The Queen's Guard
Chamber at Hampton Court, with work in progress on a
painting by Sebastiano Ricci. A modern restoration studio
is being built at St James's Palace with all the scientific
aids necessary for the proper cleaning and maintenance of
this huge collection of pictures. The outstanding
restoration work done during the present reign has been on
the great series of canvasses by Mantegna, 'The Triumphs
of Caesar', which had been considered beyond repair, but
which are now once more exhibited in The Orangery at
Hampton Court

The 'Great Piece' of Van Dyck, the double portrait of
Charles I and his Queen, Henrietta Maria, was the first
commission the artist received from the King. Because of
Van Dyck's techniques, it has always been a problem
painting, and has also suffered at the hands of earlier
restorers. In February 1980 the film cameras watched
(right) as the head of the King was cleaned, and for the
first time in many years Van Dyck's handling of
Charles I's sad countenance was revealed

Raphael: Self-Portrait (detail). This painting was given to George III as a work by Raphael, but for many years its authenticity was doubted and it was relegated to the 'Umbrian School'. However, in the light of recent research, it will be published as a Raphael in the catalogue of Early Italian Paintings in the Collection by Professor John Shearman

Canaletto: 'The Pantheon' – Detail (right) before cleaning, and (left) after cleaning

*Above: Medal cabinet by Boulle.
Left: Cylinder-top desk by F-G
Teuné, made for the Comte d'Artois
after 1781, and bought by
George IV. Both these pieces of
furniture have been restored recently
in the special workshops set up at
Marlborough House during this
reign, and staffed by highly skilled
conservation officers who specialise in
the repair of furniture and armour*

silver. They are well produced, beautifully illustrated, extremely expensive, and now excessively rare. Nearly a century of outstanding scholarly discovery in this field has now passed and the catalogues are hopelessly out of date. A start is being made on French porcelain which, it is hoped, will be followed by others on the sculpture, the bronzes, the textiles and, above all, the furniture.

This scholarship, expressed through printed catalogues, is valuable for more than the Royal Collection itself. It adds in the most vital way to the history of art throughout the world, giving scholars new and accurate tools with which to work and making them familiar with all that is present in the collections.

These catalogues fulfil another great theme of this reign – to give visibility to the collections. Time is no more favourable to paintings and drawings than to furniture. Furniture suffers mainly from neglect; sometimes paintings can suffer from too much attention. In previous centuries, the concept of how to treat an Old Master was not the same as ours. The present generation of connoisseurs want the picture to be as near as possible to the canvas that the Master painted. In the seventeenth, eighteenth and even the nineteenth centuries this was not the dominant attitude. The picture had to glow with life even if that meant a great deal of repainting rather than restoring. Some restorers never doubted their ability to improve whatever was put before them, even painting in hats or extra faces. Such changes which we should regard as outrageous were performed without criticism. Until recent times, judgement as to which Old Master painted a canvas or which bits of a painting were his depended partly on archival scholarship and, when that failed to give a lead, then on the eye of a great expert such as Bernard Berenson which, no matter how skilled, could be very personal.

Science has now come to the aid of art. Over the last fifty years, and particularly since the war, the picture restorer's art has been revolutionised and all of these new scientific materials are used when restoration work is undertaken for royal pictures. Some results are quite startling and the liberties the previous restorers took are proved to be outrageous.

There is a fine village scene by Pieter Bruegel the Elder in the Royal Collection. It is a typical Bruegel subject – rampaging soldiers are seizing goods from the village women who clutch desperately at their bundles or try their utmost to prevent the soldiers from taking their geese. It is a typical scene of pillage. However, it was difficult to place accurately in the known corpus of Pieter Bruegel's work. Subjected to X-ray examination, the picture undergoes a complete transformation. The bundle on the woman's lap turns out to be a baby, so is the bundle being torn by a

Pieter Bruegel: 'The Massacre of the Innocents'. Details (the one on the left is an infra-red reflectograph) show how the picture was repainted. The figure of a child shows through the overpainting on the left-hand detail. The bundle on the woman's lap (right) was originally another child

soldier from the mother, and even the geese turn out to be a child held up by the leg by a trooper. In fact the picture is the original of Pieter Bruegel's *Massacre of the Innocents*. The subject at some time was obviously thought to be too gruesome and the babies converted into less frightening objects of pillage; of course, a great deal of the impact of the painting was lost. Unfortunately it cannot be restored to its original state.

Recently two dramatic revelations have been made by the restorers under the leadership of Herbert Lank. George IV bought a self-portrait of Rembrandt – at first glance typical and lifelike, but on close inspection by a critical eye there were suspicious symptoms: it looked as if there had been some overpainting, but then in many Old Masters this is only to be expected. So the Rembrandt experts tended to differ, some for, some against, but a question mark lay over the picture. In 1979 the decision was taken to clean and restore the picture and subject it to a full scientific examination at the Hamilton Kerr Institute. On initial cleaning the black paint of the hat and then the cloak were soluble in the varnish remover, a situation which was rarely found in Dutch seventeenth-century painting. This seemed to confirm the opinion of one of the leading Rembrandt scholars that the face was Rembrandt by Rembrandt, but nothing else. A minute speck of paint through its whole depth to the panel was removed: when put under the microscope, each layer of paint can be discerned and

the pigments can also be scientifically assessed and, of course, compared with those from Rembrandts that are known by archival evidence to be absolutely genuine. Rembrandt always ground his pigments very finely when painting a panel and then applied the paint in very thin, evenly painted layers on a base of chalk painted over with a pale cream brown. The panel being investigated showed a chalk base and pale cream brown, but the subsequent layers were thickly and crudely painted: one aspect for Rembrandt, one against, but sufficiently powerfully against as to increase suspicion. On the other hand pigment analysis showed that the pigments could have been of Rembrandt's day – not a strong argument as these pigments were used for generations, but at least not negative.

A painting at one time thought to be a self-portrait by Rembrandt. The X-ray and infra-red pictures (left and below) show details which have led experts to challenge the earlier attribution

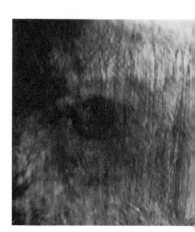

The X-ray photographs did not help in solving the problem. They showed a lack of modelling in the right cheek of the face and nose but this, again although somewhat suspicious, was not markedly different from other Rembrandt self-portraits of this period. And so, had this investigation been made in the fifties, sixties or even the early seventies, the restorers would probably have accepted Dr Winkler's view that the face was genuine, the rest painted in by a follower. But now the Dutch have invented a new instrument — the infra-red vidicon which is infinitely more complex and subtle than mere X-rays. As soon as this instrument was applied to the suspicious right cheek of the portrait, a human eye appeared. Obviously another face was below the surface. When the whole picture was carefully screened the other portrait emerged. There could be no doubt at all that George IV had bought a fake, a clever pastiche done probably in the second half of the eighteenth century when the prices of Rembrandts, particularly the self-portraits, were soaring.

But what is lost on the swings is often gained on the roundabouts. The Renaissance portrait of a young man at Hampton Court had been recently assigned to the 'Umbrian' school. This picture had been given to George III by Lord Cowper as a self-portrait of Raphael. Prince Albert, who had a passion for Raphael, had a great interest in the picture but since his day the experts have rejected the attribution to Raphael. It had, however, never been subject to scientific examination and it was badly in need of cleaning. Here pigment analysis was of prime importance for the infra-red vidicon showed that this was, indeed, one painting. There was nothing at all suspicious below: indeed from visual examination nothing was expected to be. One of the crucial factors were the buttons on the tunic which bore an inscription attributing the picture to Raphael. It was also essential to discover if the paint and the priming of the panel were treated in the manner known to be Raphael's. Six tiny specks of paint, just visible to the human eye, were taken from the picture, mainly from the edge of damage, and then subjected to microscopic analysis. The priming with its excess of glue and springy texture was typical of Raphael's grounds. The sky had been badly overpainted but what remained of the original blue was consistent with Raphael's methods both in materials, in their preparation and in the way they were used. And so the analysis proceeded: the pigments were right for Raphael, so was the use of the paint. So to the vital yellow buttons. There was no layer of varnish between the buttons and the black tunic of which they were a part, hence they could belong to the original painting and most likely did; but the black of the tunic and the black used for the

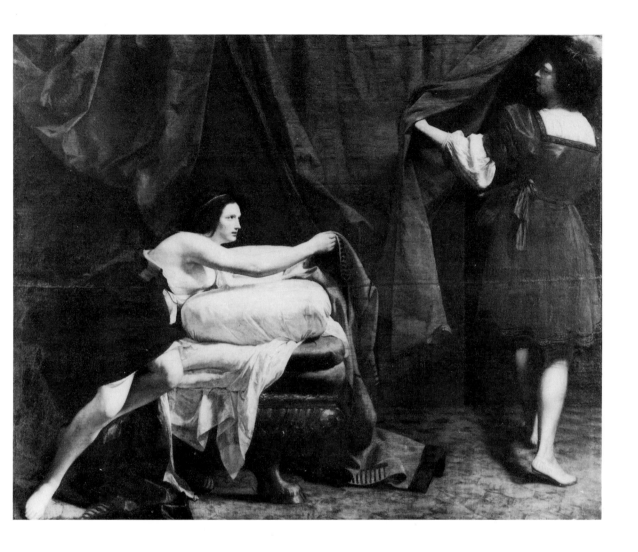

*Gentileschi: 'Joseph and
Potiphar's wife', one of the
paintings in the Royal
Collection the quality of which
is now fully revealed after
recent cleaning*

inscriptions were slightly different: the tunic was a silicate, probably umber, mixed with bone black; the inscriptions were bone black mixed with brown earth. But there was no cause for alarm, for both methods of mixing black were used by Raphael. There was no evidence at all to show that tunic, buttons and inscriptions were not painted at the same time. All the detailed scientific evidence points to an early self-portrait by Raphael. The Queen loses a Rembrandt and regains a Raphael.

What the future will turn up no one knows. A great deal of work lies ahead for picture restorers, and no doubt scientific analysis will even further improve. Some paintings are enormous: Orazio Gentileschi's vast canvas, *Joseph and Potiphar's Wife*, took five years to clean and restore. And there are pictures in the collection more enormous still. There are centuries of neglect but also, worse than the neglect, the appalling amount of excessive restoration has to be put right. But gradually the Royal Collection is appearing in all its pristine splendour, cleaned and restored to a level of which any world-famous museum would be proud; and, it must be stressed, never over-restored or overcleaned. These pitfalls, which have trapped so many museums, have been avoided.

No monarch has done so much for the collection as Queen Elizabeth II: there may have been greater collectors amongst her ancestors, but not one has taken such great care of this incomparable heritage.

The Private Chapel at Windsor Castle. Originally built for Queen Victoria, it was lined with dark oak. Recently it has been redecorated so that it is much lighter, and a way has been made through from the State Apartments to St George's Hall beyond. The Organ is a very interesting instrument designed by Willis, with a double-keyboard, and great care was taken to conserve its original pitch during its recent restoration

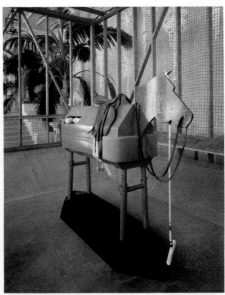

Left: Changes in the East Terrace garden at Windsor Castle (left) have included the installation of a fountain designed by Prince Philip (top left).
Right and above top: The swimming pool in George IV's Orangery with a practice horse for polo.
Middle: Drawing-Room, Edward III Tower.
Bottom: The Holbein Room, recently rearranged

CHAPTER FIVE

THE INHERITANCE DISPLAYED

Samuel Pepys always took the opportunity to look at the pictures in the galleries at Whitehall Palace when he could. He developed the habit, too, of dropping in at Sir Peter Lely's studio so that he could see portraits of the King's mistresses being painted. Pepys kept a diary so we know that he loved looking at the royal collections, but he was far from being alone in his ideas or his habits: from many other sources we know that the royal collections – at St James's Palace, at Hampton Court, at Windsor – could be seen by any gentleman. The world of authority, whether based on landed wealth, commercial enterprise or, as with Pepys, professional competence, was very small indeed in seventeenth-century England: it was almost one highly complex cousinhood. Connections, too, were often vertical as well as horizontal. Pepys's younger brother was a working tailor in the City of London, yet they were also related to the Earls of Sandwich, a relationship which they acknowledged. Usually people had connections at

The Chinese Dining-Room, Buckingham Palace, with wall and ceiling paintings newly restored by the Department of the Environment, and movable furnishings repaired by the Palace craftsmen. Much of this was designed for George IV's Pavilion at Brighton, and brought to London to create this room early in Queen Victoria's reign

court: if they were well dressed and well liked, they could go to court, stride about in the corridors, stand and talk in the public rooms, with luck catch a glimpse of the King or his intimate friends and ministers. There was usually a throng at court, and so the pictures and furnishings, the sculpture and the decorations were open and visible to a section of the population.

The eighteenth century saw a dramatic change. The well-born, like James Boswell, had no difficulty in getting to court, but the world of authority, or at least the world of social respectability, steadily grew. The middle classes, including minor professional men and women as well as skilled workers, had more leisure and more money. Had the same open-door policy been pursued by the Hanoverians as it was by the Stuarts, the courts would have been overwhelmed by curious sightseers. And from the late seventeenth century onwards, there is an increasing formality at court, a complex filtering system that prevented easy access: more and more rooms became private and closely guarded. The right to enter or to be presented to the King became much more formalised. This is often put down to Hanoverian influence, to the stiffer and more formal procedures of the German courts, but this is far from being the truth. Had the Stuarts continued to rule, the process would have been the same: the social development of the age would have forced greater regulation of court procedure.

But the public was never excluded. Royal palaces and royal collections have always been available to the public in a variety of ways. The state rooms at Hampton Court, for example, were open to the public (i.e. those respectably dressed in the eyes of the doorkeepers) in the eighteenth century. The North Terrace at Windsor was a public promenade in George III's reign and most of the courtyards of the Castle were open as well: indeed George III enjoyed strolling on the Terrace himself and chatting with his subjects. Even the private apartments might be visited from time to time by a scholar. George III used his library at Buckingham Palace a great deal – he was rightly proud of his exceptionally fine collection of books but he allowed scholars to work there: not only Dr Johnson but also his fierce radical critic, Dr Joseph Priestley. Access, therefore, to the royal buildings and collections is an age-old tradition. The problem has always been what should be available, how it should be made available, and how to retain the balance between public curiosity and privacy.

Public curiosity about royalty and the way it lives always has been intense and always will be. Indeed, public curiosity so overwhelmed Queen Victoria and Prince Albert at Brighton that it forced them to

abandon the Pavilion, the most original of all the royal residences, and build Osborne, remote and protected. But Osborne went the way of Brighton and, after Queen Victoria's death, it was given by Edward VII for use as a convalescent home and in this reign the Queen has opened the private apartments there. The curious can peer at Queen Victoria's bath and look at the bed in which she died, supported by the arm of the Kaiser. What was once utterly private is now public. In the royal life nothing is ultimately private, only temporarily so. And the intimacy revealed does far more than satisfy idle curiosity. To see the two desks where Albert and Victoria worked together side by side at Osborne, to see the great mahogany bed with the watch case waiting still for Albert's watch as it waited through the long years of her widowhood, deepens our understanding not only of Albert and Victoria but of life itself – its terrible transience: time ends for all of us and sorrow spares but few.

But there must always be a difficult policy decision about what to open and what to keep closed and private. Sandringham, perhaps, exemplifies current policy better than any other of the royal houses. The Sandringham estate was bought for the Prince of Wales by Queen

Victoria as a private family home, and private the house remained not only throughout his life and the lifetime of Queen Alexandra, who continued to live there until her death, but also during the lifetime of her successors. King George V made do, until his mother died, with the very small York Cottage (small as a house let alone a royal house – the King's study was as tiny as many an undergraduate's room). Even so he was often there. George VI was as deeply attached to Sandringham as his father and preferred to live there from October to February when the affairs of state would let him. Queen Elizabeth, the Queen Mother, also loves the house and the estate and so does the Queen. In every way it is a family home, a family estate; and is run as such.

There is a large Home Farm of some 300 acres; another 14,000 acres are let to tenants; there are 2000 acres of forest. Land has been reclaimed from the Wash where the marshes run out to the sea. The whole is farmed with the efficiency which now characterises British agriculture. The farming is mixed and there is a stud that is as well run and efficient as the farming. Even before they enter the gardens, the public can appreciate what a model country estate should look like.

The gardens were opened to the public before World War I by Edward VII – the first breach, as it were, in the most private of Royal Family houses. They were open in August and September when the Court was never there. The gardens of Sandringham are singularly beautiful and possibly at their best in late September when the autumnal colours of the foliage bring a new beauty to the gardens which were partly designed for the late summer. They attracted thousands of visitors, as did the church with its astonishing silver altar, the gift of an American to Edward VII. The gardens and the church seemed scarcely enough for the crowds that thronged there from the seaside resorts of the Norfolk coast or the industrial cities of the East Midlands. As the estate in Edward VII's day was largely a sporting estate, the King decided to create a game museum to help entertain the crowds. Nowadays the game museum speaks of an age that has passed. It is heavy with a sense of the 'Raj' – tiger skins, white rhinoceros, buffaloes, wildebeest, deer and antelope in variety, elephant. This all belongs to a time when big game was plentiful, so plentiful that there was no thought of the need to conserve and protect it which is now a very great concern of Prince Philip.

However, the advent of the motor car and its spread to all classes since World War II means that tens of thousands instead of hundreds began to visit Sandringham. And they have had to be provided with skilfully created amenities – vast car parks, lavatories, gift shops, cafeterias. One of the most instructive of the new ventures to entertain the visitors is the

Nature Trail that is walked by thousands every year. There is a short trail of three quarters of a mile and a longer walk of a mile and a half, but both give a valuable lesson in the nature of the soil of the estate and of the shrubs and trees which will grow on it. It also explains why some trees are more favoured for forestry than others. The trail is carefully designed, giving occasionally a wide view of the Wash and of the lands reclaimed from it; a piece of heathland – the typical landscape of this area – is crossed as the trail makes its way through the carefully planned forests. And the trees are alive with birds – game birds, song birds, predators, indeed birds of every variety: dozens of specimens can be seen on one walk. Sandringham indeed is a superb shooting estate and it was famous for its pheasants throughout the nineteenth and twentieth centuries. However, pheasants are no longer reared for shooting; what exist are the result of natural process, and shooting now is a necessary thinning of nature's plenitude. As the walker passes through the heather and the woods there is always a chance that he will see some fallow deer and a certainty that he will run across many red and grey squirrels – the latter are a pest and are driving out the red. The public can now enjoy the pleasures of the estate as well as the garden and learn about trees and forestry.

In addition to the Nature Trail, two excellent museums have been created – one certain to attract the young as well as the old: the museum of old cars. This has been created by the Queen and Prince Philip. The old royal cars were sold off and so many of these splendid Daimlers have had to be tracked down and bought again. The oldest is King Edward VII's Daimler of 1902, a car which can still be driven. It was a favourite vehicle of the King's, who drove it himself and indeed was frequently photographed and filmed in it. Most impressive and equally nostalgic is the great upright Daimler used by Queen Alexandra: an extremely handsome car for 1913. There is also a splendid green Daimler that belonged to Queen Mary and was owned for a time by the Nigerian High Commissioner before it was repurchased for the museum. There are two very large shooting brakes, one of which belonged to George V, the other to George VI.

As well as the old car museum, there is another that might grace any small market town. Beyond the game museum is a long, low room that contains a fascinating clutter of objects: some, like Queen Mary's china and a highly decorative collection of jelly moulds, came from the house; many are gifts to the present Queen and they all speak of affection and loyalty. Mr J. Ward presented a remarkable confection of matchsticks depicting the Coronation of the Queen – 10,526 matchsticks were used

Queen Alexandra's Daimler now on display to the public in the museum at Sandringham

in its construction which must have taken years. Not far away is a very lively and realistic bronze 'Two Champs' by Henry Jackson of a cowboy subduing a highly spirited mustang, a present from President Ford. One wall is covered by a large vitrine containing dolls: mechanical ones that belonged to George VI as a very small boy; a Highland doll that belonged to one of Queen Victoria's daughters, and dolls that belonged to the Queen or were given to her. On a wet afternoon it is hard to see the dolls for people gazing at them. There are few museums that are so artfully artless, that can engage the attention with such a variety of objects of fascinating provenance. It belongs to the age-old tradition of cabinets of curiosities.

But what the people come for now is to visit the house itself, which has been open since 1977 during the summer months. The public can walk through the saloon – almost the same as when the Royal Family is there – the television set and the football games the young princes enjoy removed, but nothing else – and so to the drawing-room and dining-room and on to a long corridor where there is a collection of sporting

*Dolls on display at
Sandringham*

guns, clearly and instructively labelled. Early in 1980, the Ballroom
was opened and will be used partly for small exhibitions – the first will
consist of photographs, many of Sandringham, that Queen Alexandra
took herself. The Queen has also made the Ballroom available for
receptions for local charities – an extremely gracious gesture to this
rather lonely corner of Norfolk. Apart, perhaps, from Balmoral, Sandringham gives a more complete picture of Royal Family life than any
other residence. It lacks the majesty and grandeur of the great palaces
but it demonstrates to perfection how a country estate should be
efficiently run and the way that the Royal Family lives when they are at
one remove from the formal occasions of royalty. And Sandringham, too,
is an excellent example of the policy the Queen has constantly pursued –
to make her heritage visible to her people. No other royal residence gives
the public such a sense of intimacy with their monarch and her family,
for these are the rooms in which she sits and talks with her family, plays
with her grandchild, and entertains her guests.

It has been a consistent policy of the Queen to open to the public as much of the royal houses and gardens as possible whilst retaining some privacy. The same policy has been pursued by everyone responsible for royal buildings and collections: a constant watch is kept for new possibilities of display to the public. Beyond the great staterooms and chapel of Hampton Court there is a small warren of grace and favour apartments. They were carved out of the kitchens, the pantries, the servants' quarters. Lady Baden-Powell, the widow of the founder of the Boy Scout movement, had such an apartment tucked into the Tudor kitchens – indeed, her bathroom was situated in the great open fireplace. After her death it was brought back into custody, the refittings of the last century removed and the kitchen restored as it was in Henry VIII's day, and it will become a new area for display. Similarly, when the London Museum found Kensington Palace too small and was removed to a far more appropriate site in the Barbican, the rooms that had been vacated were used for new areas of display. Some rooms will display costume that has been loaned to The Queen for fifty years. Court costume has not had a permanent place of exhibition so far and this will greatly enrich Kensington Palace. The Council Chamber where Queen Victoria held her first Privy Council has been restored and it now displays Victorian pictures and furniture, some of it acquired by the Royal Family in the Great Exhibition of 1851. Queen Victoria was the last monarch to live in Kensington but it was a favourite residence of William III who suffered from asthma and George I was very fond of it too, so the King's Gallery and the King's Drawing-Room have been restored – the fireplace for the latter had been moved from St James's Palace, so, most appropriately, it has been put back into the Drawing-Room. Both rooms are used to display late seventeenth- and early eighteenth-century paintings and furnishings which had perhaps not been so intelligently displayed before. The Queen and her Household are constantly looking for opportunities of this kind which enables them to put more and more of the collection on permanent view.

Although not on such a large scale as Kensington, other new display areas have been created at other royal residences. As early as the 1850s, Queen Victoria ordered that the royal apartments at the Palace of Holyroodhouse should be open to the public. Since then more and more of this historic palace has been opened. The bedroom of Mary Queen of Scots, the ill-fated cousin of Elizabeth I, has been restored to its original condition. Until recently there was only a moderate display of firearms and armour in the Grand Entrance; now what was there has been taken down, cleaned and restored and incorporated in a far greater exhibition of arms than ever before. Indeed Holyroodhouse can now take its place

Alan Carr Linford: Three watercolours from a series of views of Windsor Castle commissioned by Prince Philip
Top: View looking west over the Quadrangle to the Round Tower
Middle: View on the North Terrace
Below: Entrance to the Horseshoe Cloister, with St George's Chapel to the right

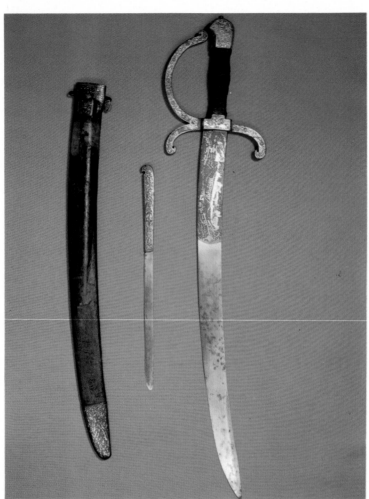

Left: Henry *VIII*'s imposing armour has long been in the Royal Collection, and stands on the Grand Staircase at Windsor Castle. Recently his hunting knives have been acquired from Italy and are displayed with the armour. They are the work of Diego de Cayas, a Spanish smith, and can be dated by the view damascened in gold, showing the King's last expedition against France, the Siege of Boulogne in 1545

Opposite: Samurai sword forged by Osafune Yasumitsu c. 1420, and surrendered by Field Marshal Count Terauchi to Lord Louis Mountbatten on the defeat of Japan in 1945, and presented by him to King George *V*I

Below: Mace with agate head, 17th century, central Europe. Used at the Court of the Winter Queen, Elizabeth of Bohemia, the daughter of James I & VI

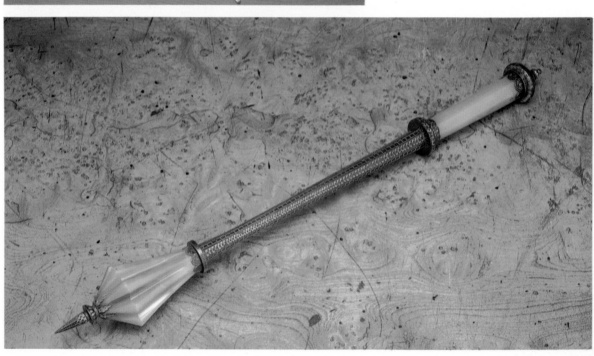

The Palace of Holyroodhouse. The recently restored ceiling of Mary Queen of Scots' bedroom

with Windsor Castle and Hampton Court as far as the display of arms and armour is concerned.

At Windsor a new glass coach house at the Royal Mews was opened in 1980 and the beautifully restored Scottish State Coach put on display along with many other fascinating vehicles. Two new galleries have been created at Windsor – one for Old Master drawings and watercolours; another for china and pottery. The drawings gallery, of course, requires special features – controlled lighting (strong lighting can quickly damage watercolours and they lose the freshness of their colour) and controlled humidity. The Old Master drawings, many of them purchased by George III and his father, Frederick, Prince of Wales, are one of the glories of the Royal Collection. They are normally housed in two rooms at Windsor Castle and they come under the direction of the Queen's Librarian. They have always been accessible to students and scholars but now they, along with the watercolours, can be shown to the public. Some of the finest Old Master drawings are always on view in this new gallery.

Sir Winston Churchill. The Queen commissioned this bust of her first Prime Minister from Oscar Nemon

165

The same is also true of the new China Museum that was opened in 1979. It is placed in the entrance lobby to the State Apartments and so engages the attention of the thousands of people of all nationalities who visit them. The display of china is brilliantly arranged in large vitrines, strongly lit in the somewhat darkened room so that the brilliant colours of the china have an immediate impact. The royal china collection from which the exhibitions are drawn is very extensive. There is a very impressive amount of Delft from the seventeenth century, probably brought over from Holland by Queen Mary II. There is an abundance of Wedgwood, some of which was presented by the founder of the firm, Josiah Wedgwood, to George III and Queen Charlotte, and a great deal, too, was collected by Queen Mary. Also Wedgwood made, specially for her, copies of eighteenth-century pieces, including many cameo portraits. There is Spode, Copeland, Rockingham in abundance, one of the greatest of all services of Chelsea, and many other factories including, of course, Meissen and the great services and vases of Sèvres for which the collection is world famous.

Although the search for new areas of display is a constant one, there are other problems that arise in the older areas. Every generation tends to take a different view of how works of art should be shown. In the eighteenth century, connoisseurs filled their walls almost from floor to ceiling: there were rows of paintings one above the other and it was a rare doorcase, no matter how lofty, that did not have a painting hanging over it. Although somewhat less cluttered, the Victorians were not averse to seeing a very great many pictures in one room – far more, in fact, than we should find agreeable today. True, in great country houses as well as in the royal palaces there are still quite a large number of paintings to a room but, as in museums, there is a tendency to give more space to a picture, to help isolate it. When it is a great masterpiece, museums tend to give it a very great deal of space. These changes produce expectations in the public as well as creating a way of looking at works of art: they are drawn to what is familiar to them. The same process has been at work in the Royal Collection. When a room is reorganised, the opportunity is usually taken to make the display of paintings and furnishings more in tune with modern taste. The King's Dressing Room at Windsor Castle has recently been rehung. It contains pictures of exceptional quality but appropriate to the room; they are all of the first half of the seventeenth century and earlier. There is the famous triple portrait by van Dyck of Charles I, the painting that was sent to Bernini so that he might model a head of the King. Bernini found it one of the saddest portraits that he had seen. There are two Rubenses – the wonderful self-portrait that was

The exhibition of Old Master drawings at Windsor Castle

purchased by Charles I and his portrait of van Dyck; Vermeer's *Lady at the Virginals* is there, and Rembrandt's portrait of an old woman, traditionally believed to be his mother, one of his great interpretations of the endurance and sorrow of age. And there are three fine portraits, Holbein's portrait of Reskimer, a portrait by Dürer and a portrait by Clouet. All of these paintings are of the highest quality and make an astonishing collection of masterpieces in a small room and one which few museums could match, but they are displayed in a way that appeals to modern taste – plenty of space around each picture, in a room in which they might have hung centuries ago, and a room, of course, furnished with seventeenth-century *objets d'art*, including the silver mirror and table that was given to Charles II. There can be no doubt that modern methods of display are triumphantly successful in this room.

Public interest in the arts has increased steadily since World War II. Far more people visit museums or country houses than attend football matches – and the appetite for special exhibitions seems insatiable. Naturally this makes demands on the Royal Collection; requests for loans are a constant feature of the Surveyors' lives. And the tradition of acceding to these requests is an old one, so long as the Surveyors can assure themselves and advise the Lord Chamberlain that the conditions of the exhibition will in no way harm the paintings or the object loaned. Indeed some paintings and objects have been placed on permanent loan at the great museums and galleries so that they can be available at all times to the public. Queen Victoria started the practice when, in 1861, she loaned a huge carved head from Easter Island, and later she lent paintings to the National Gallery. This policy has been continued by the Queen, who has placed the Raphael cartoons on permanent loan at the Victoria and Albert Museum. One of the most important early paintings in the collection is the Triptych by the Flemish artist van der Goes: this has been for some time on permanent loan to the National Gallery of Scotland in Edinburgh, and when the Queen visited Scotland in 1980, she went to the Gallery to see how the picture looked after it had been cleaned and its elements rearranged.

The greatest number of benefactions in terms of permanent loans has gone to Brighton Pavilion, which has developed a special relationship with the Royal Collection. When the Pavilion was sold to Brighton Corporation in 1847, it was stripped not only of its furniture but some of its fireplaces and fittings; some went to Buckingham Palace, some went into store, and some by one means or another were sold. After World War I, during which time the Pavilion had been used as a military hospital, the corporation took the decision to restore the Pavilion and since then it has risen, phoenix-like, from the ashes. Queen Mary became very much its patroness – searched the royal palaces for furniture from the Pavilion which could be spared, as well as the antique shops for bits that had escaped. Sometimes she purchased them and sent them to join the others which had been despatched on loan, sometimes the corporation bought them. This policy has been consistently pursued and extended during this reign and a large number of pieces of furniture and some fittings have been given to Brighton on permanent loan. Over one hundred were sent in 1956–7: indeed the Pavilion would not be half as splendid as it is without these loans from the Royal Collection.

Mostly loans are not on so permanent a basis but it is usual for a number of paintings and objects to be dispersed about the world in any one year. In 1980, an important exhibition on the Medicis was held in Florence. The Queen possessed a portrait of the Medicis' gardener, so that went, along with another painting. Drawings were also lent for this exhibition, including a Leonardo. An early van Dyck, *Christ healing the Paralytic*, was sent to Ottawa. The British Council requested the loan of six drawings for an exhibition in Munich. Brighton Art Gallery was putting on an exhibition about fairies and, of course, there was an important picture in the Royal Collection, *Undine*, by Maclise. It was soon on its way to Brighton. Hogarth's exceptionally fine portrait of David Garrick and his wife went to Stockholm. Every year pictures and drawings are sent all over the world. Loans of drawings are made more extensively than paintings – in 1979 thirteen museums benefited from this royal generosity.

A new departure took place during the Silver Jubilee year. A special Jubilee train was organised which contained a wide variety of works of art and this travelled thousands of miles across Australia, allowing men and women in the most remote places to see something of the Royal Collection. It was an immensely successful innovation.

A further development in the loan policy took place in 1976. Although the Queen had lent several pictures or drawings or objects to particular exhibitions, a complete exhibition from the royal collections had hardly ever been sent abroad. The showing of the Leonardo anatomical drawings at the Royal Academy aroused world-wide interest, and the decision was taken to send this entire exhibition abroad – to both Florence and Hamburg. In both places thousands poured into the museums to see them. The Leonardos are, of course, in a very special category, but the success of these exhibitions will increase pressure for similar ones.

Not all the increased display of the royal collections is public. One great development of this reign has been the increased entertainment in

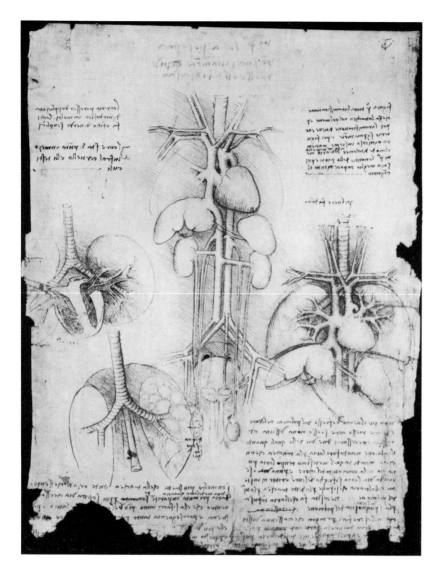

Leonardo da Vinci. Two anatomical drawings from the Royal Library, Windsor. A special exhibition of these drawings was first shown at the Smithsonian Institution, Washington DC, in 1976, during the Queen's state visit to the USA for the Bicentennial celebrations. Since then it has been seen in Los Angeles, London, Florence and Hamburg

a private way by the Royal Family of men and women distinguished in all walks of life. There are luncheon parties held at Buckingham Palace which give many people an opportunity to see parts of the Palace which would otherwise be closed to them. At Sandringham and Windsor Castle the Queen invites a number of guests to 'dine and sleep'. At Windsor where the drawings, watercolours, prints and archives are kept, special arrangements are made for these guests by the Queen's Librarian, Sir Robin Mackworth-Young. He and his staff study the guest list in advance and arrange an exhibition in the Royal Library of objects intended to be of personal interest to the guests.

At Easter 1980 the Prime Minister, Mrs Margaret Thatcher, was a

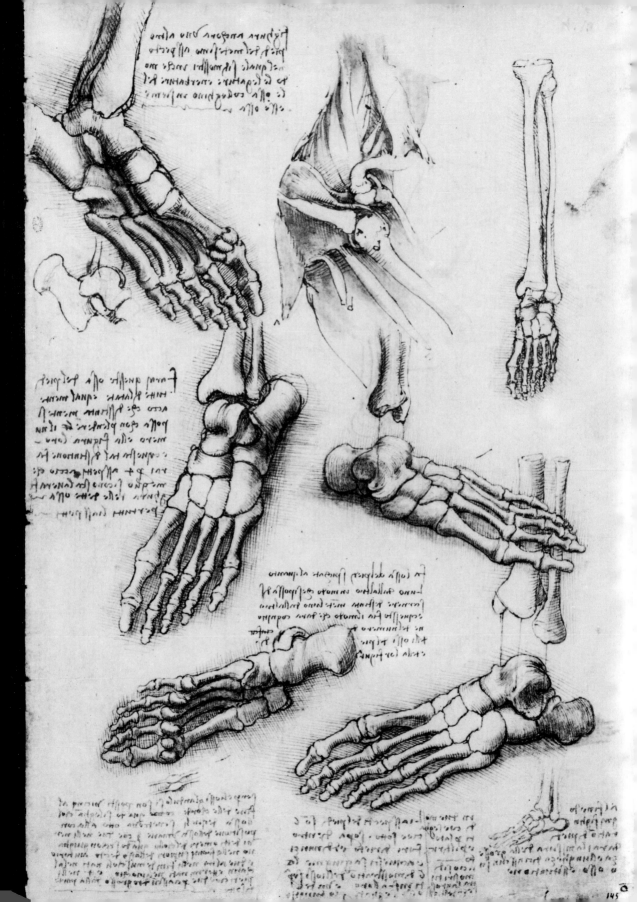

member of a party and the Librarian, knowing of her life-long interest in music, put an autographed score out for her. Much to her astonishment she discovered that it was by the young Mozart, aged ten. The Archbishop of Salzburg, disbelieving that Mozart could compose as well as play, shut him up in a room with a blank sheet of paper and the text of the First Commandment, and this was the composition that resulted. No one knows how or when the composition came into the Royal Collection. At the same party there was a biscuit manufacturer and here lively ingenuity was shown. He was shown two rolls, one baked for Queen Victoria's Diamond Jubilee, the other for the Queen's Jubilee in 1977. Another guest was a well-known film producer and for him there was a page of King George V's diary which showed that the King had seen seven films within eight days – including *The Mutiny on the Bounty*, starring Charles Laughton. The King's comment was laconic – 'too long'.

Such is the richness and variety of the Royal Collection that there is always something appropriate for the guests. There cannot be a more intimate or personal or delightful way of using the great archival resources of the Royal Collection than this. It creates interest and conversation, as well as indicating the care and thought that goes into such hospitality.

No matter how useful these various methods are of bringing more and more aspects of the Royal Collection into public view, the greatest innovation in this reign has undoubtedly been the development of the Queen's Gallery. The original building, designed by Nash for George IV, was a conservatory. It was adapted for use as a private chapel by Queen Victoria and Prince Albert. This was destroyed by a bomb on 13 September 1940 and it remained a ruin for nearly twenty years. In 1959 the Queen decided to create an art gallery on a part of the site so that the public could see masterpieces from the collection which might otherwise never be seen, or only on rare occasions when on loan to a specific exhibition. The work was completed in July 1962 and the first, most spectacular exhibition, 'Treasures from the Royal Collection', opened on 25 July. It was a great success. Consisting of some of the finest pictures in royal possession – Vermeer's *Lady at the Virginals*, Ter Borch's *The Letter*, and many others as well as Old Master drawings, *objets d'art* and furniture, it was a thoroughly representative sample of the range and depth of the Royal Collection. Nearly 6000 people visited the gallery in the first four days of the exhibition.

The opening of this gallery was as important in the cultural life of London as the opening of a new concert hall. Unlike many capital cities,

Traditionally, Royal Palaces were open to anyone who was considered presentable, like these visitors to the Cartoon Gallery at Hampton Court (left). One of the innovations of this reign has been the creation of The Queen's Gallery at Buckingham Palace out of the ruins of the Chapel bombed during the War. Every year an exhibition open to the public is organised here around one aspect of the Collections. In 1979–80 (above) it was the Sèvres porcelain, with related furniture and tapestries from French palaces acquired by George IV. In the foreground the table with a porcelain top called the 'Table des Grands Capitaines' commissioned by Napoleon

With the aid of the Department of the Environment, throughout this reign areas previously closed to the public have been opened up, and new exhibition spaces contrived. One of the earliest suites to be opened was the private rooms of Queen Victoria and Prince Albert at Osborne House on the Isle of Wight. Left: The Queen's sitting-room just as she left it at her death in 1901. In Kew Gardens, Queen Charlotte's Cottage (below), with its trellis-work decorations painted by her daughter Princess Elizabeth, has been restored and can now be visited in the summer. Right: At the Royal Mews, Windsor Castle, a new Museum has been opened to exhibit not only items such as the Scottish State Coach, but also gifts presented during Royal Tours and the Silver Jubilee

Sandringham House is The Queen's private home which can now be visited by the public during the summer. This drawing-room opens off the entrance hall

London has very few small and intimate art galleries and the Queen's Gallery filled an important gap. It is the perfect setting for the small exhibition and the policy has been to develop exhibitions on carefully defined subjects. The Surveyor of the Queen's Pictures and the Librarian, who is responsible for drawings, can from time to time mount an exhibition on a particular Master. They have done so for van Dyck, for Gainsborough, for Holbein, and in December 1980 an exhibition was devoted to Canaletto. However, there are a limited number of Masters for whom this is possible, and there is also the necessity to provide for a variety of tastes. One of the early exhibitions, in 1965, was devoted to the Queen's stamps, which delighted philatelists throughout the world. 'The Royal Review of the British Soldier' in 1967 drew on the vast resources of watercolours and prints on military topics at Windsor. The 'Animal Painting' Exhibition of 1966 exploited the great series of sporting pictures, including several very fine Stubbs, that have been acquired over the last three centuries: the range of this exhibition in time was quite remarkable. There have been exhibitions, in which the Surveyor of the Queen's Works of Art has also been involved, devoted to particular monarchs – to 'George IV and the Arts of France' and to 'George III', which came as a great surprise to many who thought of George III as obstinate, stupid and, finally, mad. He was shown to be a man of great taste, wide intellectual interests, including science and astronomy, and a collector of discernment. Every year that has passed since 1962 has witnessed a new and exciting exhibition at the gallery, and hundreds of thousands of people from all over the world have visited them. Usually they have consisted of paintings, drawings or prints – but in 1979 an exhibition was devoted entirely to Sèvres porcelain, organised by the Surveyor of the Queen's Works of Art. There was some French furniture to set off the great vases properly, and one or two paintings to take away the bareness of the walls, but these were but the setting for the greatest exhibition of French china ever held in Britain.

One of the great features of these exhibitions have been the catalogues. These are the responsibility of the Surveyors; they are models, on a small scale, of informative scholarship. The scholarship is not obtrusive; the introductions are aimed at the interested but informed members of the public whilst the detailed description of paintings and objects possess the information that would be of help to scholars in the field. Some are out of print and eagerly sought after. Indeed a real contribution has been made to the history of art as well as giving pleasure to a very wide public.

The Queen herself takes a keen interest in all the major exhibitions held in the Gallery, which is one of the great innovations of this reign and one which has made the Royal Collection available to more people than any other single development. Never before in their long history have the royal collections been made so visible to the nation at large. And the same is true of the monarchy: rarely before has the people known so much about its way of life or been so privileged to enter so many gardens, so many houses. Hundreds of thousands can now enjoy what was the privilege of a few. This has been the most distinctive feature of this reign.

ACKNOWLEDGEMENTS

We have had the assistance of many people in assembling material for this book and we should like to make acknowledgement here of our sincere thanks.

In the Royal Library and Archives at Windsor Castle, we are grateful first of all to the Curator of the Print Room, Hon Mrs Jane Roberts, for her scholarship and ungrudging assistance in finding prints and drawings; in addition we would like to thank the Registrar of the Archives, Miss Jane Langton, for information and Miss Frances Dimond of the Photographic Collection.

In the Lord Chamberlain's office invaluable help has been given by: Mr Marcus Bishop and Mr Charles Noble in the Registry; Mrs Margaret Cousland and Miss Caroline Crichton-Stuart, Assistants to The Surveyor of the Queen's Pictures; Mrs Julia Harlond, Assistant to The Surveyor of the Queen's Works of Art; and Mr Derek Chappell, senior conservation officer, Marlborough House workshops.

We are also grateful to the following for making arrangements for Michael Freeman to take photographs specially for the book: Captain Alastair Aird, Comptroller to Her Majesty Queen Elizabeth The Queen Mother; Mr Julian Lloyd, Land Agent, Sandringham; Mr Martin Leslie, Resident Factor, Balmoral Castle; Major William Nash, Superintendent, Windsor Castle.

J. H. Plumb is particularly grateful to Lieut. L. J. R. Carter of H.M. Yacht *Britannia*; Miss MacDonald, the Queen's Dresser; also Mr Arthur Benstead, formerly of Windsor Castle.

J. H. PLUMB

HUW WHELDON

THE FILM CREW

Executive Producer	Richard Cawston
Producer	Michael Gill
Director	Ann Turner
Film Editor	David Thomas
Film Cameraman	Henry Farrar
Sound Recordist	Stanley Nightingale
Film Lighting Electrician	Derek Stockley
Rostrum Cameraman	Ivor Richardson
Film Research	Shirley Seaton
Location Stills	Joan Williams
Producer's Assistant	Ann Hewitt

INDEX